1

TOO YOUNG TO DIE

BY

CHYNA

JAMERICAN:

(1) A person born on the island of Jamaica and migrated to, and living in the United States of America, while juggling both cultures.

(2) An American with either or both Jamaican parents, or other Jamaican relatives, and exhibiting a strong Jamaican cultural influence.

Before God and all mankind, I pledge the love and loyalty of my heart, the wisdom and courage of my mind, the strength and vigor of my body in the service of my fellow citizens; I promise to stand up for Justice, Brotherhood and Peace, to work diligently and creatively, to think generously and honestly, so that Jamaica may, under God, increase in beauty, fellowship and prosperity, and play her part in advancing the welfare of the whole human race.

This is the Jamaican Pledge. I can remember saying or hearing it in school, sporting events, or some other general assembly, and it is important for all Jamaicans to remember these words.

No part of this book may be used or performed without written consent from the author, except for critical articles of reviews.

PROLOGUE

"Too young to die," this phrase with its literal meaning is imprinted in Corey Young's mind. Very young, intelligent, and instilled with great moral values, Corey Young was the pride and joy of his mother's dream. His father died at the age of five, and his mother migrated to America when he was ten. At the tender age of thirteen his potential and ability to excel academically was recognized by local politicians and other statesmen who vied for the opportunity to pay for his education so they would have the claim and bragging rights to his achievements. And thus, he was selected, educated, and bred by his Jamaican countrymen to be a dynamic and significant force in their future. However, at the expressed wish of his mother he left Jamaica and went to America where his life took a drastic turn.

It was at the end of a long hot summer when Corey arrived on a night flight. The view from above as the plane anticipated landing had reaffirmed him of the beautiful images painted in his mind from stories he had heard over and over again about America, the land of opportunity, the land of milk and honey. The passage through Kennedy Airport and the ride in his stepfather's Lincoln Continental on the brightly colored lit busy streets, to his new home in Flatbush, Brooklyn, still lived up to its glittering expectations. However, the next morning sunshine exposed the facade that night had so

PROLOGUE

beautifully camouflaged. On his first walk outside his eyes beheld the ruins of an abandoned building, a homeless man rummaging through garbage, and then he stepped into some dog poop and the stench woke him up to reality. America might not be the perfect paradise that he had thought it was.

*Corey Young is now living in the Flatbush neighborhood amid the wiles of various **Jamerican** gangs and other bands of thugs of every conceivable ethnicity; all were rivals for turf and reputation.*

Faced with the challenges of a new home, a new world with different cultures and a new system, Corey Young was still confident he could be all that he wanted to be, it was instilled in him at a very young age, it was forged in the very core of his being. But the streets of Brooklyn were mean, the gangs of Brooklyn were meaner, and it wasn't long before he became a product of that environment. Corey fought, stole and sold drugs at times, succumbing to the pressures of his environment and his peers.

Years past, and so did many of the virtues instilled in Corey as a boy, the streets of Brooklyn changed and manipulated his state of mind in the name of survival. Thank God, he met and fell madly in love with Paula Smart, a beautiful girl who was significantly different

PROLOGUE

from the money hungry bimbos that he was always surrounded by. Her love and virtue changed his outlook on life, and ever since then he was always trying to live right. Inspired by Paula, and his mentor Robert Smith, Corey became determined to beat the odds, and rise above his condition; he opened a small business with a good friend, dropped the bad friends, and began making a conscious effort to live nobly and erase the stereotype that he was branded with because of his ethnicity and environment. He occupied his days with work, school, and karate classes, but there always seemed to be forces looming in the shadows waiting to sabotage is plan. It was a daily struggle, and he fought very hard, but circumstances and environment, along with his gruesome past, kept pulling him back down into the mire of the gutter that he had unintentionally dug over the years, a past that followed him like a shadow and threatened his life daily.

Corey Young was modestly handsome, six feet tall, very masculine, had black hair, brown eyes, and athletically built. He had a natural tan complexion and wore a natural serious facial expression, probably developed from his complexed and difficult childhood.

PROLOGUE

His thirst for knowledge was evident, as he would listen attentively to any advice, wouldn't dismiss anything he didn't understand, but rather questioned or searched until he finds the truth.

It is summer time, school is out, and all this free time proves to be an open door for chaos to enter and wreak havoc in his life.

TOO YOUNG TO DIE

Too young to die,

It's an incentive

Not a battle cry,

Life's so expensive

No money can buy.

Being amongst the poor

And felt the pain,

Being amongst the rich

And saw the gain.

Being amongst the wicked

And felt ashamed,

Being amongst the just

My heart got tamed.

Why go through life dying?

When you can . . . living.

You're never too old to live

Only too young to die!

TOO YOUNG TO DIE

CHAPTER ONE

"You are not in charge, you think you are, but you are not! You are just a pawn in this grandiose scheme of the so-called 'Powers That Be.' You think you control your own destiny? You don't! You're not even totally free. Once you overstep that restricted boundary you are privileged to live within, then you will start realizing who's really in charge, and that's if you are wise enough to see clearly. Long before you were born, this cycle of treacherous manipulation of mankind was put in place under the wheels of diverse political systems and their injustices. Your looks, your physique, your ethnicity, your family, your religion, and even where you're from, and where you live will all play a major role in what you will become. Sad, but true, but it doesn't have to be that way. It is true that everybody can't be lawyers and doctors, societies wouldn't thrive or even survive. Some people have to be janitors, farmers, shopkeepers, tailors, lawyers, doctors, engineers, innovators, and so on. But let us achieve our goals and our status by our own choice, by the application of our own intellect, hard work and determination. Not by deception of fixed grades in school to fail and feel defeated because one is of a different ethnic stock, religion, gender, class, or live in a certain neighborhood. So many settle for what they were led to believe they are qualified for, never challenging the status quo . . . I'm sorry, I'm just so frustrated to see so many of you brilliant youngsters falling by the wayside, because you weren't given a fair shot at life. I wonder if anybody ever stopped to think and realized that none of us, not a single one, chose how they wanted to look, or the country they wanted to be born in. But we can choose to be what we want to be, and that freedom should be every body's right. So, now I'm begging you to take heed, I love you like you are my own son, please Corey . . . stop being a pawn! Your education and knowledge is not confined to what you are taught in school. Teach yourself by using the internet and libraries.

Education is the key and knowledge is power. Make them inspire and drive you to excel and rise above the expectation that you were branded with!"

Tears trickled from Corey's eyes as he sat up straight staring at Robert Smith, his mentor, admonishing him. He's speechless . . . frozen . . . but seemed to have absorbed every word Robert Smith had just preached. Robert leaned over and hugged him, and then he finally broke his silence.

"Thanks, I needed that, you're so right, because most of the times I sit back to reflect, I often wondered why I do some of the crazy things I do. When I was growing up in Jamaica my life was so much simpler and with so much greater expectations. I was looked upon as somebody, people back home really made me feel important and loved," he said softly.

"Welcome to America . . . In Jamaica you were probably at the top of the pyramid, and I'm sure it was also because of your looks and some of the same factors that now put you at the bottom of the pyramid here in America. It shouldn't be where you are or, who you are, but what you are, and want to be, accompanied with your own dreams, hard work and determination that determine what you'll become.

CHYNA

You are a human being, a member of the human race with equal rights to pursue your dreams and coexist equally wherever you are!" Robert said forcefully as they stood up, and Corey wiped the tears from his eyes.

"You make me realize that the cards may be stacked against me, but I don't have to lose," Corey said softly.

"Exactly, stay conscious and always be aware, no matter where you are or what you're doing . . . fall asleep and you might never wake up!" Robert exclaimed.

Its 9:00 pm, time to close Sanctuary, the karate school Robert Smith runs. Corey is his number one student, and they are at the end of their usual one on one lecturing session.

"I'm going to stop by Paula before I go home, I'll catch up with you tomorrow," Corey said as he waved goodbye to Robert.

"Okay, give her my regards."

"I will."

Paula Smart is about 5' 7", with a petite body and the most beautiful smile you'll ever see. She was standing by her gate waiting for Corey to arrive, her eyes gleaming with excitement, "Ouch," She blurted out, "are you crazy?" She asked as she turned around to confront a scruffy looking guy pulling on her hair.

"Just trying to be friendly, what's your name?" He demanded.

"None of your business, you can't just pull on a girl's hair and expect her to be nice to you," she retorted puzzlingly.

"You know who I am?" He blurted out aggressively.

"Obviously not, and I don't care, just go, leave me alone," Paula cried out, and then the guy tried to pull on her arm. Suddenly, out of nowhere Corey appeared and pushed the guy away.

"You have a problem with my wife?" Corey asked angrily.

"No, but I have a problem with you putting your hands on me punk," he yelled back as he pulled out a knife and rushed at Corey with deadly intentions. One vicious kick to his chest sent his knife skyward and him whirling backwards until he hit the ground. He realized he was disarmed, outmatched, and humiliated, so he picked himself up and ran off. Paula ran into Corey's arms . . . and melts.

CHYNA

"I love you," she said softly.

"I love you too," he replied as he walked her inside.

"You know him?"

"No, he must have just being passing by while I was waiting for you. He was so rude, and I guess he doesn't know how to talk to a girl."

"I hate a man that doesn't respect a woman. He's ignorant . . . before I met you I walked in darkness . . . you are the end of my darkness Paula. This is such a rough neighborhood you live in, aren't you scared?"

"Not when I'm with you . . . my hero. I wish I could be in your presence all the time," she said with a wide smile.

"Me too, that time will come eventually, hopefully soon. You deserve a good life, and when I save enough money I will make that happen," Corey said.

"We don't need money to have a good life, as long as we have each other we can figure it out."

"It's not that simple Sweetie, we'll always have bills to pay, and if we're going to have children we'll have to have money to prepare a good future for them."

TOO YOUNG TO DIE

"I know that, I just want us to start right now, move away and then work it out together. Life here is so scary, and I worry about you constantly when you're not with me," she said softly then dimmed the lights and cuddled up in his arms on the sofa.

As Corey caressed her arm he thought deeply about her concerns. In his heart he's willing to follow her dreams now, but in his mind it's a different compromise. His overall desire is to make her happy, and he believes to accomplish that task he needs to have enough money, which he believes he can save in due time.

"My mom will be home soon," she said as she yawned.

"Okay, I'll see you tomorrow," Corey whispered as Paula walked him to the door.

"I always have a great time with you. I love you so much," she said and then they kissed passionately.

"I love you more, here, I wrote this poem for you," he whispered as he placed a folded note in her hand.

She stood by the door and watched him until he entered his car and drove off. She closed the door . . .

CHYNA

then her eyes, as she thought of their future together, imagining how she wanted it to be. However, she was well aware of the high mortality rate of the young men in their community, struggling to survive the mean streets of Brooklyn. And Corey was no exception, regardless of his ambition and drive he is still just an ingredient in this treacherous melting pot of a city. She sat on the sofa and opened the note and began to read:

MY LOVE

Long before I met you,

I knew you,

It is true,

I dreamt of you.

How you'd look and how I'd feel,

I knew you were real.

I'm blessed, my dream came through,

Your touch, your scent, your love, it's true,

Everything about you is familiar,

Even my ring on your finger.

TOO YOUNG TO DIE

No words can say exactly how I feel,

My love for you no words can reveal,

But for what it's worth,

I'll speak from my heart,

I'll die for you if the circumstance arises,

But I'd rather live and share our lives.

No matter what this life may demand,

I will love you forever and beyond.

She smiled and started folding the paper, but noticed another poem on the back:

AMERICA

You're like a magnet

With a gravitational pull like the sun,

You're like a bullet

Very fast, like when it's shot from a gun.

You attract the rich and the poor,

The desolate and so much more.

CHYNA

You stand tall above the rest,

Your riches can no one test,

In wealth, culture, and race,

You are definitely the place.

We came from near, we came from far,

By train, plane, ship, feet and car,

To beheld and gain your splendor,

Wealth, citizenship, and glamour,

You're unique in so many ways,

You've celebrated many glory days.

You have flaws, but mostly beauty,

Crossroads of the world, indubitably,

You are the land of milk and honey.

"America is a great nation, but there are extreme challenges here in Brooklyn. Gang activities and illegal drugs should raise profound moral issues. They are shattering lives and causing deaths at a mind boggling

pace. It's hard for anyone to live amongst this environment and not get affected," Paula reflected, until she drifted off to sleep.

Corey and Paula have mutual plans for their tomorrow. What will tomorrow be like? That's a theoretical question that nobody has the answer to, because there's no facts about tomorrow-it hasn't come yet. Life is a journey, and how you prepare and travel will give you a sense of how your tomorrow will be.

The sea isn't always calm, sometimes it gets wavy and rough, and so we tend to rock with the waves, because that's how we survive.

CHÝNA

CHAPTER 2

"*TOO YOUNG TO DIE*" Those are the words written on a fake license plate hanging on the back of Corey's bedroom door. It epitomized his daily concern, and it is placed in the perfect place to remind him whenever he's leaving the comforts of his home to venture into the harsh and unfriendly world, as he knew it.

It's the middle of July, 11:00 a.m., and the hot summer breeze that accompanied the projected ninety eight degrees weather failed to disrupt him from his state of somnolence. However, his alarm was more determined than Mother Nature, it rang out loud and agonizingly enough to cause him to twist and turn until he eventually gave up the fight. He tapped a button on a sophisticated instrument that glows even in the daylight, and it became silent, then he slowly opened his eyes to the sumptuous surroundings of his spacious bedroom which was walled with mirrors. He tapped a button on a remote and a large screen lit up on the wall with Patty Labelle singing, 'The best is yet to come.' He strolled to the bathroom, brushed his teeth, took a cool shower, got dressed, and about twelve he was in his driveway and about to hop into his car when Amy yelled out to him from across the street.

"Corey, hold up!"

Amy was about twenty years young, very cute, had long black hair, dark amber complexion and a voluptuous figure. She was an object of sensual delight for lustful eyes, but she wasn't too bright. She had a stupendous crush on Corey regardless of her knowledge of his girlfriend and the different women she had seen him with occasionally. She lived a whole block away, but amazingly, she was always in front of his house whenever he was leaving or coming home. Seem more like an obsession than a crush. He watched as she strutted over to him in a tight pair of black and white short set.

She was with another girl, one whom was hardly a sight to look at, a mean spirited bitch with a nasty attitude that she seemed to use to distract attention from her very pimpled face.

"Hi Amy, you're looking good as ever," Cory said smoothly.

"If you think I look good, just imagine how I taste."

"Well, I'll use my imagination for that," Corey smirked, "just passing by again?"

"I'm going by the park to jog, like I do every day. How do you think I keep this gorgeous body in shape?" She replied while gently rubbing her hands over her breasts and down and around her body flirtaciously.

"Who's your friend?"

"Oh, this is Marsha, Marsha this is Corey," she politely introduced them.

"Hi," Corey said, but Marsha didn't respond to him, instead, she turned to Amy and whispered.

"He's not all that cute like you were boasting." Her remark was loud enough for him to hear and he amused himself thoughtfully, with a smirk, *"They must have named her Marsha because she looks like a Martian."*

CHYNA

"Well, I have to go Amy, be careful, there were sightings of a spaceship hovering over Brooklyn last night," he said while cracking a smile and glancing at Marsha.

"Bastard," Marsha scowled.

"That's not funny Corey, Why don't you come and hang with us for a while? You'll see she's very nice," Amy said.

"Oh no, I have to go to work, like I do every day. How do you think I keep this gorgeous car in my drive way." He replied as he motioned his right hand over and around his car.

"He's mocking me," she thought to herself, and disappointment overwhelmed her, but she felt embarrassed only when she realized that Marsha was staring at her repugnantly. Usually she would have accepted any kind of crap Corey would dish her, and not be offended. But Marsha's presence and her obvious disapproval of her flirtation and his sarcasm prompted her to retort.

"Work, I don't believe that for one second, you're probably going to your drug spot!" A low blow, but he managed to remain calm and charming. He kissed her on her cheek and hugged her as he whispered in her ear, "You can come hang with me if you ditch your alien friend."

"Okay," she replied, very excited, and without hesitation she turned to Marsha. "I'll catch up with you later."

"Really . . . whatever," Marsha retorted then stepped off.

It's a thirty minute drive from his house to his destination, so they indulged in a little small talk.

"You shouldn't prejudge anyone you know, you've never saw me sold or use drugs, but because of my lifestyle you're always assuming. Why?"

"Because every boy around here does, it's either that or they are robbing someone, it's sickening."

"So if you think I'm that type of a person why are you so interested in me?"

"I don't know, I just know that I like you and want to be with you, I'm always thinking about you, and even when I'm asleep I'm dreaming about you. I know you have a girlfriend, but I can't deny my own feelings. Am I wrong to go after what I want?"

"No, but nobody gets everything they want, and not because it's your right to go after what you want mean its right to do it. There are other people in the equation, so somehow somebody will get hurt."

"I understand, but I'm willing to take my chances. Love is a gamble."

"Oh, so now it's love."

"I am more than just a pretty face with a hot body Corey, you will find out soon."

"We'll see, Corey replied smoothly as he pulled up into a parking space in front of C&D's Arcade, the game room he operates with his friend Danny Fields. It wasn't anything exuberant, but it yielded a nice profit that enabled them to live comfortably. Four pool tables, eight different types of video machines, a soda machine, a confectionary counter and smart operation were the elements of their success. As they exited the car Corey was greeted by a small crowd of people anxiously waiting for the store to be opened. The first thing Corey did after opening was turned the music system on, he believes that music is divine and it grabs people's attention. The right music at the right time can satisfy and comfort one's heart, mind, and soul. It wasn't long before the arcade became overcrowded with patrons looking for amusement, testing their skills, or just somewhere to hang out. Whatever their reasons they seemed to be having fun, and C&D's Arcade was the place to be. Amy looked on in awe, mesmerized at how amiable, but professionally Corey was handling his patrons. She had really thought he was just a street thug, or some kind of drug dealer.

"Hey Corey, who's the new chick?" Danny asked with a grin, referring to Amy as he walked over.

"Amy, meet Danny, my partner and good friend," Corey said as he introduced them. They smiled at each other but exchanged no words.

"I love the way the day started, looks like we're going to have a good day," Danny said to Corey, excited.

"I believe so, how's the family, it's being a while since I visited," Corey said.

"Oh, they're good. Yvonne's being kind of acting weird lately though, said she joined some group that helps the homeless. I don't know Corey, she's starting to spook me with all those late night rituals she's being doing in the basement with a whole bunch of candles. She even asked me to join her and I said, hell no!"

CHYNA

"Here comes the landlord," Corey said, looking over Danny's shoulder.

Mr. Marcus was short, fat, and scruffy looking. And his character, total garbage, the man had no scruples whatsoever. He's the perfect example of a poor excuse for a human being. With his lack of principles, and driven by an ambition to amass as much money as he possible could made him dangerous.

Wearing a grin on his face and a thirty-eight in his waist, he bulldozed himself through the crowd and yelled, "Can I see you guys outside? It's very important!"

They looked at each other disconcertingly, because he always expressed envy towards their success and tried many times to break their lease.

"Sure, come on Danny," Corey said, and they went outside immediately to meet with him; and as they approached him they could see the elation on his face and they suspected it was some kind of trouble for them.

"Well guys, today is the end of C&D's Arcade," he said sternly.

Anxiety overcame them both, but Mr. Marcus was jubilant.

TOO YOUNG TO DIE

"What are you talking about? Give it to us straight!" Danny challenged.

"Okay, you Danny boy," he said arrogantly. "You disgust me, running around here like a bigshot because you're making a couple of dollars. Your lease is up, so get all your crap off my property before the night is over. I've being waiting for this day to see you squirm and beg."

"You can't do that . . . you can't just kick us out!" Danny replied angrily, but Corey stepped between them and faced Danny. "Be careful, you know he's packing," he said in a whisper.

"I don't care, he need to be taught a lesson."

"Really . . . and you're going to do that over his place? We don't have any wins Danny, let's just pack our stuff and leave," Corey said.

"Listen to your friend punk before I show you how I really feel about you . . . dirty rasta boy, go back to Jamaica on that banana boat that you came here on, maybe you can start your own scamming business there, punk." Mr. Marcus said arrogantly, and threw a copy of the least at Danny's feet and begins to walk away.

Danny was fuming with anger, and so was Corey who stopped Mr. Marcus in his tracks.

CHYNA

"What's the matter, you don't like Jamaicans; you think we're all scammers? America is the biggest scammer in the world. Check your history, in 1974 when American economy was in trouble, Nixon sent his aides to Saudi Arabia to pull off maybe the biggest scam in the history of the world. Ever heard of the Petrodollar? Google Petrodollar. They promised the Saudis weapons and protection if they only use US dollars in their oil trades. Over time the Saudis stockpiled hundreds of billions of US

dollars that America just printed and shipped, and the only way to spend it was to invest it back into American businesses and buy US Treasuries. Decades later when they sell back those Treasuries they get little

interests that didn't even keep up with inflation. They work hard through blood sweat and tears to get the oil out of the ground, and America just trade them for a promise and phantom money; and because of that deal

the US dollar also became a global standard. And let's not talk about how they got Manhattan from the Indians for $24 worth of trinkets and beads. Get the full story

and you'll understand what I'm talking about. You disgust me, and I'm glad we're leaving." Corey exclaimed.

Danny wanted to act off his anger, but Corey was able to keep him in check. Business was good, and they were having so much fun enjoying life, they probably forget

they didn't own the place. Danny was hurt, so hurt that

tears began to stream down his face. Corey had no real responsibility, but Danny had two young children and a wife depending on him, and now his only source of income is cut off suddenly. Corey tried to console him the best he could.

"Look Dan, it's not so bad, we can find somewhere else and start all over again. This is just a minor set-back."

While wiping tears from his eyes, and nose running, Danny replied, "Easy for you to say, you don't have a wife and two kids to take care of, I do. What am I going to do to support them? It's not just me Corey, it's my wife and kids. I love them so much."

"I know, and I love them too, you guys are like family to me, and I'll be here for you guys no matter what."

"I know that, but it's my responsibility. We need to find somewhere fast and open up another shop."

"That's the spirit, let's go straighten out our affairs and talk with our patrons. They should know what's going on."

"Okay." They went back inside and Corey explained the situation to Amy and then convinced her to take a cab home because he won't be leaving until late. Amy understood and complied; she didn't put up a fight even though she wanted to stay with him.

Danny seemed demoralized, the way Mr. Marcus handled him was cruel. Corey, however, seemed unfazed, calm and cool, as if losing his business wasn't a big deal.

It was about midnight, and they closed up shop for what they realized will be the very last time. Simultaneously, they both uttered the same word as if they had rehearsed together for this moment, "Bye."

Then they stood and stared at the storefront for a moment, as if they were waiting for a response.

On their way home Danny called his home and learned his wife and kids had already went to bed. He then suggested they stop at a diner and grab a bite and cool off. While waiting for their order they reminisced about the great times they used to have at the arcade. Suddenly, three thugs wearing masks and armed with double barrel shotguns walked in and announced:

"This is a stick-up, everybody on the floor!"

Everybody scrambled to the floor without hesitation. The thugs emptied the cash registers and everybody's pockets with no problem, but then one of them pulled up a young girl from off the floor and started forcing himself on her. He was trying to kiss her while rubbing his hands all over her breasts. Nobody dared to say or do anything, but Corey could see the anxiety on Danny's face, and he knew he wanted to try to help the girl, so he kept nodding his head and making facial expressions begging him not to. But Danny couldn't take it any longer, so he jumped up and grabbed the guy away from the girl and punched him dead in the face. The guy fell on his butt, and without hesitation he fired once and Danny was thrown back against the wall . . . blood squirted everywhere. Corey lunged towards the shooter but slipped on the bloody floor. The shooter then got up and stood over Corey aiming his gun dead at his face and pulled the trigger, but just a click; his gun appeared empty, and he said in a deadly tone: "It's not your turn to die today!" then ran off with his accomplices.

Corey rushed over to Danny and discovered he was already dead. He closed his eyes and embraced Danny's body for a moment, then walked out of the diner and sat in his car, deep in thoughts, and crying. Suddenly, he screeched off, flooring the gas pedal all the way to his house.

In the confines and secrecy of his home he grieved for almost two hours then decided to go by Danny's house.

CHYNA

It was about three in the morning when he rang the doorbell several times and waited patiently for about five minutes. Mrs. Yvonne Fields, Danny's wife, answered the door. Suspiciously she asked, "Where is Dan, is he alright?"

"Can I come inside?" Corey asked sadly.

"Sure," and as if reading his mind she asked, "You bring bad news, don't you?"

Tears begin to trickle from his eyes, and seeing that she started shaking her head and crying.

"No, please don't tell me something bad happened to him . . . please?"

"I'm sorry, I'm so sorry, he was helping a little girl in trouble and he got shot . . . he was killed.

Corey spent the rest of the morning trying to console Mrs. Yvonne Fields and her two children, he even let her know that she could depend on him for any kind of help she may need. But her grief seemed to consume her whole being. She and the kids just curled up in the sofa sobbing, and wouldn't react or respond to anything he said or done. They seem to need this time to be by themselves, and Corey needed to grieve by himself too, in private, so he said his goodbyes and left. But as he stepped outside he muttered, "Oh, I feel so dizzy."

He stumbled to his car and sat for a while to catch his breath, then called Paula and told her about the tragedy. She broke down in tears, but was happy Corey was fine. The thing she dreaded most is coming too close to home.

"That could have being Corey, and my whole world would have being shattered," she thought.

Death seemed to cause more pain to the loved ones left behind, than to the recipient.

The first few days Corey inquired about Danny's case to no avail. His killer seemed to have disappeared in thin-air, and no leads to who or where he is. Nobody seemed to be cooperating with the police or, were they investigating? Whatever the case, there was no information available and every road he took led to a dead end.

CHYNA

Is death a part of life,

That ends this physical strife,

Where pain and misery disappear,

And your body just lay there,

Decaying, or vanished in thin air?

Or is death just the beginning,

Of a new life unending,

Living in misery that is endless,

Or living in ultimate happiness?

TOO YOUNG TO DIE

CHAPTER 3

With the death of his business partner, Corey seemed to have sunken into a deep emotional and physical depression. He picked up a bad gambling habit which was more of a stress reliever and recreation to him, rather than a means of making money. But he was always winning, sometimes over a thousand dollars in one night. The four men he gambled with were all in their twenties, so winning all this money from them regularly was astonishing, until he learned they were into drug dealings, extortions, and robberies. The type of bad company he had shed from his past. They were all Jamericans, so it was easy for him to relate to them. Corey didn't always enjoy their company, because he despised their cursing, smoking, and drinking habits. However, winning their money and their humor allowed him to tolerate their negative dispositions, which he usually would shun. They were always talking about their lavish lifestyles, and how fast and easy they made their money, and how much respect they get from everybody. All their gloating seemed like a plan to induce Corey into their way of life, a life that he had known and long left behind, but Corey appeared too intelligent and uninterested to fall into their snare. He never once partook into their smoking or drinking, but he would listen to their stories and laugh at their jokes. He thought Lou was funny, and Ron despicable. Ron would brag often about his dalliances with other men's wives, and did it proudly.

"Most of the guys I robbed were because I got in bed with their women, true, no lie. And the funny thing is, they are usually happy to help me rob them," Ron said arrogantly.

"So what makes you so special, you have the magic stick?" Lou joked, and Corey smiled.

"Maybe, but one thing I know is that I'm giving them what they aren't getting at home. Think about it, their man work hard busting their chops sometimes twenty hours a day, piling up all that money and not taking care of their bodies. They don't eat right, don't get enough sleep, and don't have time to talk to their women much less make love to them the right way. They just can't satisfy them, and that's where I come in."

"So you're a predator of some kind?" Corey asked.

"Yeah, Joe Grind," Lou joked, and everybody laughed. "These women aren't too smart if they help you to rob their own husbands or lovers who are bringing home the beacon."

"Yeah, why kill the goose who laid the golden egg? You better be careful about these women, you might soon become a prey yourself, because these women you're attracting don't seem to be thinking straight," Corey said.

"You guys are just jealous, I'm making a career out of this," Ron said seriously.

Several weeks of intense gambling, almost every night, seemed to be taking a terrible toll on Corey's mind and body. It's about two in the afternoon and he's struggling to get out of bed. Finally he did, and stared into the mirror and saw a zombie staring back at him. He realized he can't go on living like that, hardly eating, hardly sleeping, neglecting Paula, and hardly doing anything but gambling. *"Ron might be targeting my woman, damn, funny how you can get knowledge in the strangest places,"* he thought to himself. This was no way for a man of his caliber to live, and he didn't want to become one of Ron's victims, he seemed to realize. So he took himself a long hot bath and decided to cook himself his favorite meal: brown stewed red snapper with rice and peas.

Corey looked into the mirror again and the zombie had disappeared. He picked up his phone and speed dialed, and an alluring voice answered, "Hello."

"Hi Sweetie, I cooked our favorite meal, brown stewed snapper with rice and peas, and it's all set up with candle lights. I miss you," he implored.

"You sound precarious."

"Yes, and also insatiable, do I have to come and get you, or, are you already on your way?" He cooed.

TOO YOUNG TO DIE

"I'm already on my way darling, just walk slowly to the door and you might find me waiting. By the way, what's for dessert?"

"Your favorite."

"I'm not so sure you remember what that is."

"Are you kidding, after all those dinners we had together?"

"Okay, just for the record let me hear you say it."

"Okay, I'm your favorite dessert Sweetie, and you can have me any way and with whatever topping you desire."

"Forget about walking slowly to the door, run as fast as you can," she said, and hung up the phone in a hurry, which left a wide smile on his face. He dimmed the ceiling lights low enough so that the candle lights became dominant, and then placed a dozen red roses already in a black lacquer vase on the center of the table. He pressed a button on a remote and the sweet enticing voice of Barbra Streisand threatened to steal the moment as she softly croons notes that touched his soul. Luckily, he noticed Paula standing in the doorway. She was breathtakingly beautiful, dressed in a red satin dress and flaunting a smile that made Mona Lisa looked like a bull dog. He was startled by the quickness of her arrival, but her lusciousness prompted him into a state of obliviousness. He stared for a moment, then attempted

to speak, "How did you . . ." but she stopped him, "Don't say another word, just come and welcome me," she said softly, striking a pose that revealed curves that Jennifer

Lopez would've been jealous of. He wasted no time as he embraced her and kissed her passionately while

Streisand sings: 'My heart belongs to you.'"

She responded like butter on a hot skillet, melting in his arms as he swept her off her feet and carried her into the bedroom. He opened her dress and stared on her beautiful nakedness while a pleasant smile formed on his face.

"I love you," she breathed softly with watery eyes, and he proceeded to have her his way, with her full and delighted cooperation, all the time enjoying the sensual look on her face as she gasped in delight.

Wallowing in contentment, they gave each other immense satisfaction as her earth-shattering climax and cry of fulfillment sent him over the edge as well. And as his hot sweaty body shivers she embraced him tightly, waiting for their breathing to return to normal. And after a brief rest she spoke, "I thought dessert was supposed to be after dinner?"

"That was the main course and dessert in one," he answered jokingly.

"Funny, because now I'm twice as hungry," she chuckled and closed her eyes.

Sex is a behavior that quenches thirst, anger, hunger, frustration . . . you name it, but only for as long as it last.

Since the beginning of time sex has been used as a catalyst, from the simplest to the grandest of endeavors to accomplish both ignoble and noble goals. It's the most satisfying feeling, and should be shared and enjoyed out of mutual love and respect, not to be used to hurt others, for self-gratification, or to topple kingdoms; but people will be people.

CHÝNA

CHAPTER 4

The sunshine came piercing through the mini-blinds and on to Corey's face, but it's the heat that it emits that forced him to open his eyes to the dawning of a new day. Only eight thirty and it's already eighty five degrees and is expected to reach ninety eight by three. He rolled over and realized he was alone, the goddess he had spent the night with had vanished, and the only trace she left was the erotically and satisfying memories of last night. He somehow made it to the bathroom and refreshed himself with a nice cool shower.

TOO YOUNG TO DIE

His brain begins to function and life seemed worthwhile again, so a significant objective for the day is necessary. As he began to contemplate an agenda he was interrupted by the doorbell. A pleasant expression overshadowed his face, expecting to see the goddess that had deserted him last night, but when he opened the door it was Ron, one of his gambling buddies.

"Oh, it's you," Corey said disappointingly.

"Yea, it's me, who did you expect, Publishers Clearing House with ten million dollars?" Ron replied amusingly.

"No, I wasn't expecting anybody."

"Hard to tell, the way you swing that door open wearing happiness all over your face."

"What do you want Ron? I'm through with gambling, so there's no reason for you guys to come around here anymore, okay?"

"I didn't come here to gamble, I'm here to offer you a chance to make some quick no risk money." Corey stared at him with suspicious eyes, then blurted out,

"Really, who do I have to rob or kill?" Corey asked with sarcasm.

CHYNA

"All you have to do is drive me to Long Island, wait about fifteen minutes then drive me back and I'll pay you four thousand dollars. "

Corey was puzzled, "Do I look stupid? A taxi driver would probably charge you about fifty bucks and save you a whole bunch of money. Why don't you ask one of them?"

Ron stared at Corey dumbfounded, trying to figure out if he's really stupid, and Corey continued to insinuate.

"Oh, I get it, you're going to rob a bank and I'll be the get-away driver, right?"

"No Corey, listen, it's my uncle's house, and I know where he keeps his money and a briefcase filled with gold and diamonds. He's a jeweler, and sometimes he brings home his work."

"You're gonna rob your own uncle?"

"Come on, don't get self-righteous on me now, he can afford to take the loss, plus him have insurance."

"Man, you are cruel."

"Man, it's a cruel world we live in. So, are you in or what?" Ron asked sternly.

TOO YOUNG TO DIE

"If it's as easy as you say it is?"

"Trust me, if it wasn't a sure thing I wouldn't even think of doing it."

"Okay, I'm in, but all I'm doing is driving, nothing else!"

"That's the deal. Pick me up at ten tonight, but call first."

"Okay, I'll be there."

Ron was pleased, and so he left. And Corey begins to lament in his misery. The chance to make a quick and easy four thousand dollars impaired his judgement badly. His conscience begins to manifest to him his weakness. In is solitude, physical signs begins to express his emotions as he paced the floor blurting his thoughts out loud.

"This is so wrong, suppose we get caught and I go to jail, what will my mom think of me? What will Paula think of me? What will Robert think of me? Then again, how can I get caught if all I'll do is drive him there and back? Four thousand dollars, that's a lot of money for doing practically nothing, and in less than an hour."

He realized he's talking to himself, so he looked around, then hit himself on his forehead with the palm of his right hand and blurted out, "I'm going crazy?"

CHYNA

To Corey, the day seemed unusually long, passing by in slow motion as he wrestled mentally with the different scenarios playing out in his mind for ten o' clock tonight. He became weary and drifted off to sleep.

Hours passed by, the sun disappeared and the darkness that always accompanied night seemed to come later than usual. It's now nine thirty, and Corey is hesitant to call Ron as planned. Anxiety momentarily subdued his whole being, but he somehow forced himself to pick up the phone and dialed.

"Hello," Ron answered before the end of the first ring.

"Hi Ron," Corey replied in a gasp.

"I thought you changed your mind."

"Me too, I'm on my way though."

"Okay."

The five minute drive to Ron's house felt like forever to Corey as his mental torture continued, even after he picked him up. He followed his direction to his uncle and parked around the corner from the house. "I'll be back in about ten minutes, don't leave," Ron said forcefully, and Corey listen attentively while reclining his seat to lay low. He waited nervously, and in less than ten minutes Ron was back with a briefcase and a small duffle bag. He opened the suitcase and gave Corey a peek, and his eyes flickered wide open with excitement, and they began to celebrate with high-fives and laughter.

But as they drove back they became quiet, and so terrified thoughts came flooding into Corey's mind.

"I hope he don't get greedy and try to renege on our deal, dang, I hope nobody saw us. I can't deal with any heat right now," he thought to himself.

"Can I crash at your house tonight? It would make things easier. This way I could give you your money tonight."

"Sure, it's late anyway," Corey replied.

"Great, I don't have any privacy at my house."

"So how did you get in the house?'

"Oh, I have a set of keys."

"I guess you're a suspect already then."

"No, I opened a window and turned over some plants and trash the house a little so they'll think somebody broke in."

CHYNA

"Whatever happened I didn't bring you, and after tonight please don't come back to my house."

"You don't have to worry about that, I'm going on a long vacation in Jamaica, I miss my homeland."

"I know how you feel dude, there's nowhere like home."

"Yeah, I'll be lying on the beach every day, no problem."

"Sounds great, I should be thinking about doing that too, the best memories I have are of when I was growing up in Jamaica. It's been a while though since I've been back."

"Well, I think you should just do it, you can afford to."

"I think I will . . . oops, we're home."

It's almost midnight and they eased into the dark drive way, no one in sight, but they took the back door entrance just to make sure there were no suspicious eyes watching them.

"Piece of cake, I told you it was easy," Ron blurted out as he opened the briefcase and emptied it on the table in the living room. Loose diamonds and gold jewelry sparkled as Ron combed his fingers through them in delight.

"Well done," Corey said with a smile.

"Oh yeah, you don't see anything yet . . ." Ron reached for the duffle bag and emptied it, "this is my retirement."

Corey stared in dumbfounded amazement as Ron count the bundles.

"How much you think is in there?" Corey asked.

"I'm guessing about a hundred grand, could be more though."

"Wow, I think you should leave, I'm getting real nervous."

"Okay, no problem, I understand . . . here" he said and handed Corey the four grand he had promised him.

"Thanks."

"That's it? You're not going to ask for more?"

"We made a deal and you kept it, I'm good."

"Here anyways, they're untraceable. That's about ten grand if you sell it to the right person," Ron said as he handed Corey eight pieces of the diamonds.

CHYNA

"Thanks, but I don't know how to move this."

"Take this number, its Lou's, the same Lou who gambled with us, tell him I send you whenever you're ready. You can trust him."

"I think you should disappear tonight, unless you have somewhere good to hide all that stuff for a while. I wouldn't underestimate your uncle if I was you."

"Corey, I'm protected. I'm in this club that protects me even from the police. If you want, I can hook you up to join, just say the word."

"Na, I'm good. I'm not a good follower."

"You have no idea what's going on right before your eyes, these people took the blindfolds off my eyes and showed me a whole new world. You can be a part of that world anytime Corey, just say the word."

"No thanks, like I said, I'm good."

"Call a cab for me, my plan is solid, just take care of yourself and keep this between me and you, okay?"

"No problem, I'm on it." "Can I use that big suit case you have over there, and give me some old clothes too so I can camouflage the money and jewelry."

TOO YOUNG TO DIE

"Sure, let me check it first to make sure there's nothing in it to lead back to me," Corey said smiling.

"Hurry up, the cab is here."

"Okay, go ahead and pack your stuff, I'll go make sure the taxi stay put."

"No, don't go out there, he won't leave, and I'm just about ready."

Corey peeked through the blinds as Ron packed the suitcase in a hurry.

"Alright, I'm out," Ron said and offered Corey a handshake.

"Be safe," Corey said while he shook his hand.

"Thanks, you too," Ron replied and head out the door.

As the taxi pulled off, Corey locked his door and took off his shirt then blurted out a big sigh of relief. His imagination begins to run wild trying to figure out how his tomorrow will be. But his phone rang and startled him. It was Paula apologizing for leaving while he was asleep this morning without waking him, because she had to go to work. After they hang up he was intense in his thoughts, but his body was weary, and so he drifted off to sleep.

Corey is brilliant, and like many of the young men in his community, he needed motivation. Good opportunity was scarce because of the environment, but it was bad company and unfortunate circumstances that deceived many of them into bad situations that often times yielded negative consequences. The mentoring he had received from Robert Smith which usually resonated through his mind when confronted with a dilemma seemed to have lost its relevance. Corey seemed to be slipping!

TOO YOUNG TO DIE

CHAPTER 5

Five in the morning and the cool breeze that accompany this time hit Corey on his bare chest and caused him to quiver. And the bright light from the ceiling add more agitation as he carefully tried to open his eyes. With his eyes half opened he searched for his shirt and tripped and hit his head on an ottoman. Relieved that he's not hurt he refrained from killing the object that tripped him. He noticed that the object was the bag that contained his take from last night and he suddenly realized how he had ended up half naked and sleeping on the sofa. He took advantage of his early wake up to get an early start on the day by taking a shower and make some breakfast; then allowed Streisand's exhilarating voice to relax his mind as the sun rise to give the morning a warm welcome.

It was about eight o' clock when the phone rang.

"Good morning," Corey answered.

"What's up Corey?" Ron asked in excitement.

"Nothing much, I'm good. I see you're still here."

"I told you I'm protected, stop the worrying, I already called Lou and tell him to expect you."

"Oh great, I'll call and set up a meeting."

"Okay, I'm out."

After Ron hang up the phone Corey contemplated if he should get rid of his diamonds now or wait. "*Holding on to these diamonds is not just memories, but evidence to a heist that could yield serious consequences,*" he thought, so he dialed Lou's number.

"Hello," Lou answered.

"Hi Lou, Ron told me to call you about some diamonds I have to sell."

TOO YOUNG TO DIE

"I don't know which asshole is this on the phone, but you obviously got the wrong number and the wrong person!" The next sound in Corey's ear was a click. Lou hangs up the phone without warning or explanation. Corey was stunned and he began to realize it might not be a good idea to get involved with Lou. He knew the type of people who deals drugs are often ruthlessly greedy and violent. He was so shaken up by Lou's attitude that he thought about stashing the diamonds and just canceled the whole thing. But again he thought about the money it could bring him, and he began to talk to himself, *"I know I had the right person and the right number, that was Lou's voice. Why did he talk to me like that? I must have said something wrong. By the way, even if I said something wrong that chump didn't have the right to dis me like that. Wait a minute Corey, you're beginning to sound like a thug."* He realized he had just stepped out of character, and not just this time, but many times before.

"Check yourself Corey, check yourself, and don't let him get to you." (Speaking of the devil)

Corey Young was nurtured in a Christian family back in Jamaica, but since he came to America many of his virtues have withered away with time and negative environment, but his moral compass was not totally shot.

CHYNA

Robert Smith was a good mentor to him, and had managed to help him to see goodness in himself, and that the choices he makes will determine what he will become.

"Don't let your anger cause you to sin," he thought to himself as he tried to settle his nerves. Later the doorbell rang and he went and answered it.

"Hi Ron, come on in, you have just save me a trip and some time."

"Oh yea?"

"Yea, your punk friend Lou . . . sorry . . . I mean, your friend Lou just totally dissed me on the phone."

"Yea, I know, that's why I'm here."

"You know?"

"Yea mon, you was wrong and he had no choice."

"I was wrong, I spoke to him like a gentleman, and I even told him good morning."

"Yea you did, but gentleman can also end up in prison."

"Now what are you talking about?"

TOO YOUNG TO DIE

"Okay Corey, listen to me, and listen carefully, people like me and Lou, and even you now, is in a business that attracts the law . . . you know, like the police, feds, DEA . . . you know why? Because our business is illegal . . . and so we have to be real careful with every step we take, especially with the phones. The phone is their best watch dog and it never sleeps. Get the point?"

"Yea, I get the point, but what does that have to do with him dissing me?" Ron looked at Corey in wonderment, tempted to call him stupid but refrain because he knew he was a rookie in the business. He kept his calm and tried not to make an already bad situation worst. "Corey, think about what you said to Lou on the phone this morning, word for word."

Corey remained silent for a minute in his thoughts.

"Damn! Damn! Damn! I feel like a fool, I was talking about selling him diamonds, and I even called him by name. He must be real mad at me." "Sure he was, but he doesn't hold you fully responsible anymore. I'm partly to be blamed since I had told you to call him without prepping you. I should've known better to set up a meeting instead. If you don't mind, he would like you to bring the stuff at this address nine thirty tonight."

CHYNA

He handed Corey a piece of paper with the address and anticipated a positive response which he got without hesitation or question.

"Thanks Ron, tell him I'll be there."

After Ron left, Corey fixed himself a cold glass of orange juice and once again allowed Barbra Streisand's exhilarating voice to serenade him while he regained his composure. He thought about female companionship, but nine thirty kept ringing in his ear.

"Will there be any risk or danger? Sure, there is always risk of prison and violence when dealing with shiesty individuals," and as that thought entered his mind he jumped up from out the sofa he was lying in and silenced Streisand. He picked up the phone and called John. John was a straight-up guy he knew he could trust, even though they only played soccer together every Saturday. John was an ordinary looking guy, twenty four years old, dark skinned, five feet eight inches tall, and about a hundred and seventy pounds. He didn't look intimidating, but Max thought his presence could give him some comfort.

"Hello," a male voice answered.

"Can I speak to John please?"

TOO YOUNG TO DIE

"This is John, who's this?"

"Oh good, this is Corey. I need to see you today about something which I don't want to discuss on the phone. Are you busy?" Corey asked, remembering the lesson he had just learned about telephones, how it could be his worst enemy.

"I'm having lunch right now, but in about twenty minutes I'll be free."

"That's perfect, you want me to come by you, or would you prefer to come over by me?"

"You can come get me."

"Okay, I'll see you about twelve."

John lived about twelve minutes away from Corey but he decided to leave immediately. As he was about to open his car door he was startled by an annoying voice, "Hi sexy!" The car keys fell out his hand and he spun around to face his nuisance. "Amy! You startled me," he replied with a tinge of smile, trying to hide his acerbity. And Amy responded in her usually sensual, yet annoying manner.

"Oh Corey, not you frightened by little bitty me, I'm so sorry."

CHYNA

"It's okay, my mind was somewhere else."

"That's nothing new. Whenever I'm in your presence your mind always seemed to be somewhere else. Are you afraid I might steal your mind? It's your heart you should be worried about."

He already knew Amy's intention, and her approach is an everyday event in his life, one he can't seem to shake. He knew he had no time to waste with her, but didn't want to hurt her feelings, so he offered her some satisfaction.

"Would you like to go for a ride Amy?"

"To where?" she asked, as if it really mattered. She would go with him anywhere at any time, and he knew that too. So he answered with sarcasm, yet humorously.

"To hell, get in the car!"

"Okay . . . don't be so pushy, I have to get back home soon."

"Don't worry, you're in good hands."

She couldn't pass up the opportunity to murmur a humorous lewd response.

TOO YOUNG TO DIE

"I've being dying to get into your hands to see what you can do."

"What?"

"I said I know I'm safe in your hands," she replied smiling.

"Oh, I thought you were getting smart again."

"So, where are you taking me?"

"I'm just going to see a friend, you mind?"

"No I don't, just as long as it's not one of your girlfriends."

Corey found a parking spot directly in front of John's house and eased in.

"I'll be gone fifteen minutes the most; can you wait in the car until I get back?"

"Sure, just leave the radio on."

"No problem."

John saw them pulled up, so he greeted Corey at the door before he could ring the bell.

CHYNA

"You're early, who's the cute chick in the car?" He asked.

"That's Amy, my neighbor." "Your girl?"

"No, she's just a friend."

"So what's up, can I have her?"

"Not mines to give, let's just take care of business, okay?" Corey replied in discord, showing signs of resentment.

"Okay, okay . . . so, what's so important?"

"I have some diamonds I'm taking to sell somebody tonight, but I don't feel too comfortable going by myself. That's where you come in. I'll give you three hundred dollars just to follow me."

"Three hundred dollars, sounds like you don't trust whoever you're dealing with. Who are they anyway?"

"Lou."

"Lou . . . The Lou who drive the black Benz?"

"Yea, you know him?"

"Not personally, but I know of his reputation, everybody in Flatbush know about him."

TOO YOUNG TO DIE

"You think I can trust him?"

"Trust, when it comes to money you should trust no one, don't you ever forget that. Give me five hundred and a gun and I'll go with you."

The five hundred is no problem, but I don't have a gun."

"No problem, what time?"

"I'm meeting him nine thirty."

"Okay, come get me about eight thirty so we can talk some more and get prepared," John said with a tinge of excitement.

"Alright, here's my cell number in case you leave the house."

"Okay, be cool . . . aye, what about . . . you know . . . Amy?"

"Another time."

Corey returned to the car where Amy was waiting patiently, hoping that he would spend some time with her after he finish conducting business.

CHYNA

"That was quick, what's next?" Amy asked with a wide smile.

"Home, but I'm stopping by the gas station first . . . that's a very peculiar ring you have on, and why is it on your big finger?" He asked as he noticed a gold ring with an emblem of some sort on her big finger.

"Isn't it? It's my father's, but he doesn't know I have it. I just stole a wear."

"Is your father really a judge?"

"Yeah, so you better treat me right," she replied with a smile.

They stopped at the first gas station they saw and parked by a pump.

"You want anything, like gum or something to drink?"

"A soda," she answered.

"Any particular flavor?"

"Surprise me," she replied.

"Keep the doors closed," Corey said to Amy, then hurried pass a group of guys hanging out in front of the store.

TOO YOUNG TO DIE

"Maybe I shouldn't leave the car running," he thought to himself. Amy's engine was still running too as she sat in the car with great anticipation that Corey will fulfill her fantasy today. So many times she'd try to bed him with no result. He was always busy or with someone else, or maybe he was just being evasive. She didn't seem to care. No matter what or when, where or how, she's just happy for this opportunity.

Corey grabbed two cokes and went to the counter, then pulled out a stack of hundred dollar bills, peeled one off and handed it to the cashier. As he did, one of the thugs outside noticed and informed his friends. They then began to take positions, but Amy was watching and realized Corey might be in trouble.

She turned off the engine, the car engine that was, hers was still running. She took the keys out and went into the store to warn Corey.

"Corey, they are waiting for you outside, it looks like they are planning to jump you."

"Who, what are you talking about?"

"The guys you passed on your way in, it's about four of them."

CHYNA

"Oh yea, okay, stay in here and don't come out until I call you out, okay?"

"Okay."

Corey stepped out of the store cautiously, but fearless. He's confident that four thugs is no match for him since he's skilled in karate. As the door closed behind him two of the guys confronted him, one had a knife, and he did all the talking.

"All we want is your money, and you can keep your life!"

Before Corey could respond he glimpsed two other guys sneaking up behind him.

"Come on fellas, nobody will get hurt if you'll just back off and let me keep mines, I'm not the one you want to mess with."

The thugs looked at each other and smiled as if they were amused by his response.

"Oh, look who we've got here, a super hero, and a funny one at that."

TOO YOUNG TO DIE

They all began to laugh out loud and Corey knew it was the perfect opportunity to strike. First he kicked the one with the knife on his arm and the knife fell.

"Oh shit! He broke my arm, you're dead punk!"

They tried to rush Corey, but every time they rushed towards him he sent them flying backwards with a fist or a foot in their faces. Amy and the cashier looked on, and so was a crowd of people who heard the thugs screaming in pain.   Corey dismantled the four thugs and transformed them into sissies in less than a minute. Amy ran out to hug Corey and give him a big kiss, and then he realized his mouth was bleeding. They jumped into the car and rushed off.

"Need to get home quick and stop this bleeding," Corey said softly.

Amy was flushed with excitement, palms sweating and her engine racing in overdrive, and entertaining only one thought, *"Need to get home quick and stop this aching."*

Five minutes later they pulled in the driveway and Corey opened the door then ran straight for the bathroom with Amy in hot pursuit. He gargled with cold water, stared in the mirror and realized it was nothing to worry about.

CHYNA

"A little bruise, that's all," he said, as Amy appeared behind him and wrapped her arms around him.

"I'm glad you're fine, I was so scared Corey," she whispered softly in his ears. He stiffened up for a brief moment, but her minty warm breath had sent a thrill straight down to his toes, and he could feel her shivering body pressing up against his.

"It's okay, I'm glad you're here to help me through it," he whispered as he turned around and began kissing her. She kissed him back and it became evident that they both wanted the same thing, to devour each other. In the past he was able to resist her, but at this moment he seemed to be mesmerized sensually. He undressed her aggressively, and she wasn't afraid, she could sense her long awaited fantasy was about to be fulfilled. She willingly surrendered, and tears of joy began to fall from her eyes as he pleased her. She moaned and gasped, her legs quivered while digging her fingers into his back. He didn't care, it's a sensual pain; all that mattered was the fire that she had ignited in him. Exhausted blissfully, they cuddled while they recuperate.

Emotion is a natural instinctive state of mind deriving from one's circumstances, mood, or relationships with others. It's one's sense of feeling, sentiment, passion, sensibility, sensation, love, and even hate. A conflict of emotions can impair one's judgement, but lust is usually the culprit when sex is involved. Why is it so hard to resist this carnal desire even when you know it is wrong; even when one's moral compass seemed to be in place?

CHÝNA

TOO YOUNG TO DIE

CHAPTER 6

The exhaustion after great sex that usually put one in a state of somnolence didn't seem to affect Corey. He had eight thirty on his mind and he was well aware that it was already eight. Amy was out cold and lying on top of him. He knew it was time to get ready to pick up John, so he tried to pull himself from under her. The friction of their bodies aroused him sensually and the thought in his mind was overridden by the one from his erection. He skillfully helped himself without objection or rejection as a warm smile of approval formed on Amy's face. He rushed himself to a quick orgasm knowing that time did not permit foreplay nor after-play.

Elsewhere another event that would have a tremendous impact on Corey's life was taking shape. Lou is planning an ambush to rob Corey of his jewelry. He's arming his henchmen, about eight of them, with guns and knives. If you rob another crook don't expect the police to come knocking on your door. The same person you rob will be gunning for you, snitching was supposed to be against the street code. And Lou was well aware of that.

Corey's phone went off and John's number appeared. His adrenaline begins to flow rapidly and his discomfort becomes evident to Amy as she stared at him puzzlingly.

"Hey John, I'm on my way."

Amy realized her time is up, so she got dressed in a hurry and followed Corey's lead. Neither of them said a word to each other. She was satisfied, and knew he was too, and she didn't want to spoil that. After all, she's looking forward for more moments like this and didn't want to chance jeopardizing it. She walked behind him nonchalantly to the car. Surprisingly, he opened the passenger door first and let her in. She was so touched she whispered to herself, *"He's not as cold as I thought."*

Then she reciprocated politely by saying, "Thank you," with a smile. He didn't say a word, but the smile and look he gave her speaks volumes, and that was enough for her. He stopped in front of her house and said, "I'll call you," and that too was enough for her.

TOO YOUNG TO DIE

"Okay, I had a real good time with you," she replied softly as she backed away from the car.

She watched him as he vanished around the corner, then she closed her eyes as if hoping and praying that he wouldn't vanish forever.

John was looking through his window as Corey pulled up in front of his house, so he hurried outside.

"You're ready," Corey asked delightfully.

"Sure, since eight."

"We're still early, with about half an hour to kill."

"Let's go by Prospect Park and chill for a bit."

In five minutes they were in the park, and parked in an isolated area near the lake. John pulled out a nine millimeter handgun.

"Look," he said, as he showed Corey the gun, "this is all the insurance we'll need."

"Great, but let's hope you don't have to use it."

"I'm just dying to use it, and I hope some asshole try something stupid."

"Oh no, I just want to get rid of this stuff and get out of there as fast as I can. No shooting!"

"What if I don't have a choice, that's why you're taking me right, to make sure everything goes smoothly?"

"Yes, but I know the guy and I don't think he'll try anything."

"Okay, you're the boss, no shooting unless it's necessary, and I'm coming along for the ride just in case, right?"

"Right . . . and you'll get your money no matter what!"

"If you get killed, so will my money, so I'll make sure you don't, by any means necessary!"

He held up the gun to his face and kissed it in admiration. His words and confidence in his gun erased all the discomfort Corey had about nine thirty.

"Let me see that," Corey said, and held the gun for a minute then gave it back. The gun was very seductive, and he became more relaxed and asked John if he had another gun.

"You have another gun I can borrow?"

John looked skeptical.

TOO YOUNG TO DIE

"What?"

"Another gun . . . just in case."

"No, and if I did I don't think I would give it to you."

"Why not?"

"Because you might accidentally shoot me with it."

They both burst out laughing, and that was the beginning of a new friendship.

"Believe it or not, I actually know how to use one, maybe better than you, Corey said smiling.

"Really, I doubt that, and what if you kill someone, once you do that there's no turning back." John replied.

Their time spent in the park brought them remarkably closer together, so nine thirty was now more of an adventure, than of risky business. The time to meet Lou was drawing near, so they left and entered a huge abandoned junk yard on Avenue D with caution. No one was in sight, but the silence and darkness mixed with the spooky surroundings of old cars made them feel suspicious. Corey looked at John and says, "let's forget this."

CHYNA

But before John could respond a car pulled up alongside them. It was Lou, and he was by himself. He got out of the car and signaled them to follow him.

"To where?" Corey asked.

"To my office," Lou answered.

They followed him to an old trailer where the only lights in the junk yard could be found. Corey was well at eased by now thinking he only had Lou to deal with if anything goes wrong. But John was still very cautious and was looking in and around every corner and old car they passed by. The moment they entered the trailer Corey opened his bag and show Lou all the jewelry.

"Here, beautiful, aren't they?"

Lou looked at them carefully and replied, "They are beautiful, so how much do you want for them?"

"I was thinking eight grand, they worth much more."

Lou kept rocking his head silently, as if contemplating some kind of negotiation, but he was also looking towards a window as if he was stalling and waiting for someone. John suspected he was up to something and swiftly interjected, "I know someone who will give you the eight grand Corey, let's go."

Lou was running out of time and patience so he drew his gun, a big rusty .45, and said, "Okay, I'll take it, only I'm not paying for it!" He said forcefully.

"I know you were up to something!" John blurted out.

"Shut up, you piece a crap!" Lou screamed as he raised his gun to knock John in the head. Corey quickly realized, and his karate skills is about to come in handy for the second time today. He raised his right foot with lightning speed and kicked the gun from Lou's hand, and then he kicked him repeatedly in his face until he hit the floor in a bloody stupor.

"You greedy fool, now look at you, you look like a piece a crap!" John yelled at him as he picked up the .45 and handed it to Corey.

"Now you have your own gun, even though you don't need it. Man, you were just like Bruce Lee," raved John as he jumped around imitating Corey in karate stances.

CHYNA

They tied up Lou, and picked up the jewelry. Then John noticed another bag and checked it.

"Well, well, well, look what I found," John said excitingly. "How much is in here?" He asked Lou.

"Six grand," Lou uttered.

"You're lucky we don't kill you chump," John said, and spit in his face, "forget you know us, or I'll come looking for you."

"Leave that money John, and let's go, I don't need this problem," Corey said.

"Are you kidding me, this punk was about to rob and kill us, and you want to show him mercy."

"Not mercy, I just don't want to start something I can't finish."

"I'll finish it right now," John said as he aimed his gun at Lou's head, then suddenly shots rang out and broke through the window.

"Shit . . . weh we a go do now? We trapped." Corey blurted out franticly, as his Jamaican accent begin to surface for the first time.

"We have to rush out of here blazing, you ready?"

TOO YOUNG TO DIE

"Just say when," Corey replied.

"What about him?" John asked looking at Lou.

"Just leave him, if he come after us we'll make sure he regret it."

"Okay, but we're taking this money, on three . . . one . . . two . . . three!"

They kicked the door open and ran out with guns blazing and dashed for cover behind a junk car. The shooting stopped, but the air was saturated with gun smoke.

"We've got to get to our car," John said calmly.

The sounds of sneaky footsteps grabbed their attention so they point their guns in that direction and waited for the right moment. As John saw a figure appeared he fired twice hitting one dead in the face, and as he fell to the ground Corey saw another one positioning himself to shoot John, so he quickly sprang into action with a dropkick to his head. One kick was all it took and he was out for the count. John looked at Corey gratefully, but wondered why he didn't use his gun instead. There was no time for arguments or questions, more punks were on their mind and the shots that began ringing over their heads kept them reminded.

CHYNA

"I have a plan," John said.

"I'm all ears," Corey replied.

"I'll cover you and you run to get the car."

"Why not the other way around?" Corey asked.

"Because I know I'll kill any one of those punks in a second to save your life. And I'm not so sure about the other way around."

"Okay, whatever you say, I'll be back," Corey replied.

"I know," John said with a friendly smile.

As Corey sneaked off to get the car John got busy firing rapidly at the punks. Corey made it to the car with ease and raced back for John amidst a hail of gunfire. He screeched to a halt and swung the door open next to John who dove in as one of the punks ran towards the car. John took the .45 from Corey and squeezed off three at the punk sending him sprawling to the ground. They screeched off leaving bodies, a trail of dust, and the echoes of gun shots behind, not to mention some very pissed off punks. As they raced towards home they could hear the sounds of sirens coming towards them, so they slowed down. As the police cars raced by them they began to worry about the aftermath, and Corey's Jamaican accent resurfaced again.

"You think them a go snitch pon we, you think them a go call we name?"

"No, I don't think so, they won't give up the satisfaction of getting us themselves. We have a war on our hands now though. The police are the least of our problems," John explained.

"But they are the ones who violated us, we just defended ourselves."

"True, but they won't see it that way. Corey, when dealing with guys like Lou all morals are out the window, its kill or be killed. They will do anything necessary to have things their way, even kill their own flesh and blood, especially when money is involved."

"Oh boy, I guess I'm getting more than I bargained for, I don't want to kill anybody, this is the kind of life I swore to stay clear off."

"I understand, but if you have to defend yourself you won't feel as guilty. You do what you have to do, and you move on. Remember your own words: You're too young to die!"

Back at the abandoned junkyard the fleet of police cars arrived at the scene that just minutes ago was like the "Gunfight at the O K Corral." Except, now it's deserted with the scent of gun smoke and three dead bodies scattered in the dark. Lou, and who's left of his gang had mysteriously vanished before the police arrived.

As Corey pulled into his driveway a thought hit him.

"Damn, you think Ron have anything to do with this?"

"Who's Ron?" John asked.

"He hooked me up with Lou."

"I don't know, you know him, you should know."

"He robbed his own uncle. I think we should pay him a visit."

"We?" John asked facetiously. "Corey, my job is done, here's your half of the money if you want it.

"Thanks, it's not worth the trouble, but since the trouble is already here, kudos . . . Listen John, you and I know that this is not over, and we're in it together. We really need to figure out a way to end it or even stop it from getting worse."

"Okay, okay, I'm sorry. I was just playing with your head. I wouldn't leave you alone in this mess, plus, I get a high from dealing with punks like Lou."

"Okay, let's go pay Ron a visit."

"Wait Corey, let's put away the money and jewelry and then go by my house to get some bullets."

"Alright, sounds like a plan."

They stashed the jewelry and money in Corey's house, and then stopped by John to reload their guns. Now they're ready for Ron, and so they head straight over there. John had one intention, to dust him off.

It was midnight when they pulled up in front of Ron's apartment and everything seemed normal. The front door to the building was locked and disappointment overcame Corey, but John came to the rescue as he pulled a bunch of keys out of his pocket.

"Don't worry, Mr. Locksmith is here."

CHYNA

Corey looked at him wryly, but remained patient and silent as he checked out the lock on the door, then searched for a specific key from his bunch.

"This should do it," John whispered as he inserted and turn the key. Click, and the door opened on the first try.

They made their way up the stairs towards Ron's apartment. They didn't know if he's home or have company, and John seemed very anxious. He believed they were double-crossed and justice had to be served, and served the traditional thug way:' you violate you die.' He was evidently excited about the upcoming event and Corey looked at him in awe, then said capriciously, "John, I don't want to kill him, I'm not even sure he has anything to do with this."

"Okay, what if he's guilty?"

"Then he's all yours."

John smiled, knowing the odds are . . . he is.

As they approached Ron's door they pulled out their guns and Corey made a suggestion.

"Back me up."

TOO YOUNG TO DIE

"Back you up, what do you mean by back you up?" John asked whimsically.

"I'm going to kick the door in," Corey replied.

"Hold up man, you watch too much television shows," John said humorously as he pulled out his keys and stepped to the door. Corey knew that was a much better idea so he allowed John to use his skills without any interruption. Thirty seconds later the door was opened to a dark and eerie hallway. They heard voices and realized Ron had company . . . much company, by the number of voices they could hear. But the voices sound weird, like a chant of some kind. They looked at each other knowing they had to devise some sort of plan.

"Let's sneak up and see how much people we have to deal with, it sounds like they are all in the same room," Corey whispered.

"Okay, then what?"

"Just follow my lead, okay?"

They carefully sneaked up and were flabbergasted by what they saw. Men and women, about sixteen of them, robed in black hoodies formed around a circle chanting a weird language that they couldn't understand.

CHYNA

"Let's get out of here," Corey suggested.

"Right, let's go."

They sneaked back out and closed the door behind them and head back down the stairs.

"What was that all about?" John asked.

"I don't know, but it seemed like some kind of cult meeting. Did you feel that heaviness inside the apartment?"

"Yeah, and there was a musky stench, if we had stayed a minute more I would have puked," John replied as they approached the front door of the building.

"Holy crap, isn't that Lou ringing the doorbell?" Corey asked in a whisper.

"Yep, that's him, and it's three of them, and they're coming in," John replied as he pulled out his gun, and instantaneously Lou saw them too.

Lou and his henchmen reached for their guns and Corey and John dove to the floor. And without hesitation John fired his nines with precision, sending Lou's henchmen reeling to the floor riddled with bullets. Lou realized he was now alone and no match for the opposition, so he ran off. Corey was staring at John, astonished, and then finally uttered some words, "Where did you learn to shoot like that?"

"Experience like this," he chuckled as he got up off the floor.

They hurried out the building and screeched off in the darkness as the familiar sound of police sirens was speeding towards them. "I recognized somebody there," Corey said.

"Who?"

"Yvonne Fields, I'm sure it was her. My friend Danny's wife, just before he got killed he told me how spooky she was becoming. Something really sinister is going on in this community and it's getting real scary."

"I don't know, but as long as I have my gun I'm not worried. I keep it loaded and ready."

"That was probably your sixth body tonight, this is getting too serious," Corey murmured.

"Better them than us, plus it was self-defense," John replied in justification.

CHYNA

"I don't know what to make of this whole thing . . . you think Lou was going up by Ron, and for what?"

"I don't know, and at this point I don't really care. From now on I'm shooting first."

"Don't you always?"

Corey phone begins to ring and he noticed its Paula, but he didn't answer.

"It's my girlfriend, you mind if I pick her up before I drop you off, she's just around the corner."

"No, go ahead, I'll come by tomorrow, and be careful because Lou is very pissed off."

"He's probably still running scared."

They began to laugh out loud remembering Lou, how he took off when he saw his friends dropped out next to him. Corey stopped in front of Paula's house and honked his horn and she came running out.

"Why you didn't answer the phone?" She yelled.

"I was just around the corner when you called Sweetie, and I was longing to see your beautiful face and those juicy lips . . ."

"Oh Corey, stop, save it for later, I'm going to get my bag."

"Okay, I'll wait for you, hurry up."

"Okay," she replied and ran back inside.

"Damn John, close your mouth!" Corey said, noticing his lustful eyes undressing Paula.

"I'm sorry, I just couldn't help it. She is gorgeous."

"Forget it, by the way, thanks for everything tonight."

"It was just business," John replied.

"No, it was more than that, and you know it too. You saved my life a couple of times and I will never forget it."

"You saved mines too partner."

"I totally respect your gun game . . . you remind me of me when I was your age," Max smiled and stretched over to give him a hug.

Paula was staring at them with a quizzical look on her face.

"I guess you don't need me tonight," she said jokingly.

CHYNA

"Don't be silly," Corey replied with a smile. She got in the car and five minutes later they dropped John off at his house. As they neared his home Corey pulled out his gun and carefully looked up and down the street. Paula was a little frightened but didn't even bother to question his behavior. They went inside and he sighed, and the relief was also evident on his face. "You just can't be too careful nowadays. Too much people getting killed for nothing," he said, trying to justify his demeanor.

"I know, you can't be too careful," replied Paula. Corey headed straight for the bathroom and into the shower. Paula wasted no time in joining him and a long awaited and well deserved shower was interrupted, but with no objection. After the shower episode they struggled to the bedroom latched into each other's arms. "Darling, I'm worried about you . . . I'm worried about us, it's time to move away and start a family," Paula said softly. "I know Sweetie, that's my plan."

"Are you sure? because as much as I love you, I will always choose life over death, and life over love. Like those words on the back of your door, the very words that reminded you every time you walk out this room, I am too young to die . . ." she whispered while she drifted off to sleep in his arms.

TOO YOUNG TO DIE

CHAPTER 7

7:30 am, and the cool morning breeze gushed though an open window striking Corey on his face and caused him to toss and turn until he knocked over a figurine that woke him up. He opened his eyes to discover the goddess he had spent the night with had vanished once again. But the sweet aroma of blueberry pancakes and fried eggs coming from the kitchen put a smile on his face and a different thought on his mind. As he rolled of the bed Paula walked in with a tray packed with blueberry pancakes, fried eggs, fried plantains, freshly squeezed orange juice and a cup of cinnamon blend tea.

"Oh no, get back into bed darling."

"That's for me?"   "Yes darling, breakfast in bed, I know you had a rough night."

CHYNA

"That I did, but let me go use the bathroom first."

"Okay," she replied, then hopped back into bed and began daydreaming. She yearned for a happy future together with Corey, but she's a realist, and she accepted things for what they are. Brooklyn is a melting pot of diverse people and cultures, crime is prevalent, and police brutality is on the rise. Being young, impressionable, and confident can easily be mistaken for rebellious. To escape the trap of this environment and achieve her goal, she knows it will take determination, a constructive effort, and collaboration with Corey.

Corey returned from the bathroom and hopped into the bed next to her and began kissing and caressing her.

"Go eat your breakfast first before it gets cold," she mumbled, yet responding sensually.

Corey didn't reply, "Never mind the food getting cold," he thought. She's hot and in heat, and he didn't want her to get cold, so he continued to arouse her and she responded sensually.

Even if they wanted to stop they couldn't, the climax set by the heat of the moment as they kissed and caressed each other was beyond their control. So they delighted themselves in another voyage of sexual gratification.

Half an hour later, and well spent, somebody finally spoke.

"Corey, why do you carry a gun?" Paula asked in a whisper.

"I'm too young to die! I'm just too young to die darling. I have to keep reminding myself of that because I have so much to live for, and you are my number one reason."

"Somebody wants to kill you?"

"Maybe, but there's nothing to worry about, everything will be alright."

"You don't know that, the way life is in this city, tomorrow is always uncertain. We need to start thinking of a way out, and I don't necessarily mean the city itself. I'm talking about life, the way we're living it from day to day, all we do is talk. We need to start our life together."

"I know Sweetie, but there's so much going on with me right now. After I sort this out, then we'll make that move together . . . I promise."

CHYNA

"As much as I love you I won't wait forever. This city can be a trap if you tread it blindly. I'm so tired of seeing my brothers and sisters falling victim to the status quo, and I don't want you to be next, so hurry up."

"I will Sweetie, I will," he said bemused, then reached for the tray of food and satisfied his stomach.

The phone rang and Corey answered.

"Hello."

"Hi Corey."

"Good morning, what's on your mind?"

"Can I come over now?"

"In about one hour."

"That's fine, I'll see you then."

"Okay, bye."

Minutes passed by and Corey noticed Paula was silent, so he turned his head and saw that she had drifted off to sleep.

For several hours Lou was off his mind until John called. Now it's time to prepare for the beginning of a new lifestyle. Unfortunately, not the one Paula proposed. But one that will involve violence without limits, and chances beyond measure. He is well aware, but he's also aware that it comes with the territory of being a thug. He knows he's ensnared by his association with bad company and love for money, but he's in much too deep now to half-step . . . six bodies deep. Even though he didn't kill anyone he knows he's just as guilty as John, and even Ron. Those thoughts were haunting him and tears began to trickle from his eyes. He went into the bathroom and dropped to his knees and began to pray: "Father, forgive me please, I'm sorry, I messed up big time. You know I'm not a wicked person, but look what I've become overnight. Stop us from getting any deeper, please. I'm too young to die."

The tears began to fall more rapidly and he opened his eyes to see Paula standing in the doorway crying. They embraced each other in consolation, quietly, but were disturbed by the doorbell.

Paula went back to the bedroom and Corey went to answer the door.

"Hi John, come on in."

"Good morning, you had breakfast yet?"

CHYNA

"Yes, at a matter of fact, I did."

"Is Paula still here?"

"Yes, anything else you want to know?" Corey asked amusedly.

"No."

"Okay, have a seat in the living room, I'll be right back," Corey replied and then went to the bedroom.

"It's John, what are your plans for the day?"

"I don't have any, what are yours?" she asked sheepishly.

"If I tell you I'm afraid we might never be the same."

"Don't you think I deserve to know?"

"Yes, but you might hate me afterwards."

"Then don't tell me, just change them . . . let's make our own plans and move on from here."

"It's not that easy Paula, just give me a chance to clean up this mess I'm in, and then it will be just me and you . . . please?" He implored.

TOO YOUNG TO DIE

"I'll get dressed, in the mean time you can decide what's more important to you. No matter what, I'll always love you," she said softly and head for the closet.

Guilt overcame him, and he held down his head and went into the living room, but his countenance changed when he saw John.

"So what now partner?" Corey asked.

"Well, let's get rid of the jewelry first."

"What about Lou?"

"Don't worry about him, let him worry about us."

"You mean just relax and let him come at us?"

"No, never relax! Then he'll catch us off guard. You want to go find him and kill him?"

"No!"

"That's what I thought, but if it's up to me that's what I would do, then that would be the end of our troubles. Listen Corey, life is cruel and people die, sometimes good and sometimes bad. We are not bad because we are doing what we have to in order to survive, " John replied bluntly.

CHYNA

"I'm tired of the killing."

"Tired? You haven't killed anyone yet!" John replied in a high tone.

"Keep it down, will you. I don't want Paula to know about this," Corey whispered.

Corey believed John is right, but his morals were rebelling against that concept. His life is fast slipping into an uncontrolled downward spiral of crime and indecency. In a sense, at this very moment, he's faced with a critical life changing decision. On one hand Paula represents the good he aspires to be, and on the other Ron represent the bad that he consciously detests and wants to flee. But environment, circumstance, and peer pressure is proving to be a catalyst that he cannot shake.

"I'm ready," Paula said with teary eyes, as she walked out into the living room.

"You want to wait until I come back, or you want to come for the ride?" Corey asked John.

"I'll come for the ride," John answered, and Paula realized Corey had made his decision, and so the tears began to fall.

"I'll work it out Sweetie, I promise," Corey said softly as they walked out the door.

"Corey!" Amy yelled, as she crossed the street over to them in a hurry.

That annoying voice that sounded so familiar halted Corey in his tracks, and then John looked at him with a smirk.

"I smell trouble," he said.

Paula stared into Corey's face and asked, "Who is that?"

"A friend," he replied, and then turned to Amy to try and stop her advance.

"Amy, can I call you later, I'm in a hurry."

Paula suspected his intention and intervened quickly.

"Hi, I'm Paula, Corey's fiancée. Who are you?"

Corey was stunned, and so was Amy, so he quickly spoke before Amy could open her mouth and start a fight.

"I told you she was a friend!"

CHYNA

"I asked her, not you," Paula retorted, "well, I know you can talk, I just heard you call out his name," Paula said, staring at Amy intensely, and Amy finally decided to calm or cause the volcano to erupt.

"I love him," she said indignantly while staring in Corey's face.

"But I don't love you, and there is nothing going on between us, and there never will. So you need to step off now," Corey replied bluntly.

Amy was embarrassed, and began to cry as she walked away without saying another word.

"What is it that made you men think that you can have your cake and eat it too? Does it make you feel powerful, because actually, it makes you weak; I've put my life on hold for you because I love you, I wanted to spend the rest of my life with you, and I thought we have a plan; I am a strong woman, and my goals will not change, either we do it together, or I'll do it by myself, or with someone else. Either way I'm going to make it happen." Paula said sternly, while she stared down Corey who remained silent and stone-faced.

On their way to Paula's house the tension between her and Corey was evident, and so John tried to ease it.

"I admire you Corey, you didn't flinch when it was time to defend your girl, even though you were hurting that bitch feelings. That is true love!"

Paula looked at John with disgust, but silent, so did Corey. They stopped in front of Paula's house and she got out and slammed the car door, and then walked away in frenzy without even saying goodbye.

"Damn, you should learn how to control your women. You lost two in one day," John said with a grin.

"Small thing, she'll get over it."

"Yeah, but what about you, she seems like a keeper. My grandmother always says, 'if you find someone you really love, don't let anything get in the way.' I'm still waiting to find that someone; and it seems like you already have."

"Yea, I think so, she means everything to me, but I'll have to sort myself out first."

"What about Amy?"

"What about Amy? I don't even know why she's acting like that. There's nothing serious between us."

CHYNA

"Too bad she doesn't see it that way, at least that's not the impression I get from the way she looked at you."

"Just drop it, okay? We don't even have time for that." As they pulled up into the driveway John saw Amy walking up to the car.

"Well, you better find some time now, because here she comes again."

"Oh snap!" Corey blurted out. And as they got out the car Amy pushed Corey and began yelling.

"You two-timing son of a bitch!"

"Hold on. I did not two-time you, and my mother is not a bitch, so watch your mouth."

"I'm just a friend, right, that's what you told her. Well, tell me now!"

Her ranting and raving caused the neighbors to begin looking through their windows.

"Can we talk about this later, please? I have something to do right now," he pleaded angrily, and went inside with John, closing the door behind them.

Amy must have felt belittled and embarrassed again . . . she just walked away.

"Wow, women, I can never understand them!" Corey screamed and stomped his feet in frustration.

"Can't live with them and you can't live without them," John said, trying to support Corey's feelings.

"Whoever first coined that phrase knew exactly what they were talking about," Corey said while proceeding to the kitchen, and then asked, "You want something to drink?"

"Sure, I'll have a beer?"

He helped himself to a glass of orange juice and gave John a beer then they sat in the living room to discuss business.

"I have a buyer for your jewelry, but he won't pay you what you want for them. But I think we should just sell him and have one less problem to deal with."

"Okay, I just hope he doesn't turn out to be another Lou."

"No, I know this guy personally."

"That's what I said about Lou, can we do it now?"

CHYNA

"Sure, we can go by his house if he's home. Let me call and find out."

"Sure, go ahead."

John reached for the phone and dialed.

"Hi Jose, can I come by and bring that thing we talked about earlier?"

"Sure, I'll be home."

They grabbed the bag with the jewelry and Corey noticed John had his gun on him.

"Why you have your gun on you?"

"Because it's the only way I feel comfortable. I'm not going to get caught out there helpless. You can depend on your karate skills if you want, but I guarantee you, you'll never be going to my funeral."

Corey stared at him in deep thoughts, then went and got his gun too.

"That's smart thinking kid," John said.

It only took them twenty five minutes to reach Jose's house.

"You want to come upstairs with me?" John asked.

TOO YOUNG TO DIE

"If it's alright, but you know I trust you, right?"

"I know . . . come on."

They went through the open front door and ran up two flights of stairs. John knocked on Jose's door and was greeted by three beautiful half naked girls.

"Hey, you guys here to party?" One of them asked with a seductive smile.

"Maybe," John replied smiling back.

"Business," Corey said as his eyes wandered around the room while they followed behind the girls to meet Jose.

Latin music was playing, alcohol was everywhere and orgies were taking place right before their eyes. Jose was sitting between two naked girls counting money while puffing on a big cigar.

"Hey John, go get a drink for you and your friend, and join the party. You know how we do here, pick any girl or man you like and . . . whatever," Jose said in a rather rambunctious attitude.

CHYNA

"Okay," John said, but noticed Corey's disapproval, then turned to him and plead, "do not insult him, just get a drink."

"No, I didn't come here for that. I'm leaving," Corey replied forcefully.

"Okay, okay . . . relax. I'll take care of it. Give me the stuff."

"Let's just make a deal and get out of here, I'm getting a funny feeling," Corey said as he handed John the bag.

"Jose, we can't stay because we have another engagement. Here's the stuff we talked about," John said and gave the bag to Jose.

"Okay, your friend don't want to party, I understand. But you come back later, okay?"

"You know I will," John replied smiling.

"You know I'll have to check it, right?"

"Off course, go ahead."

Jose pulled out a kit and began testing and weighing, and after about ten minutes he made an offer.

"I'll give you sixty five, I have to make something off of it," Jose said.

After a brief stare, Corey smiled and agreed.

"Okay, you have a deal."

"You guys sure you don't want to party?" Jose asked.

"No thanks, we have some other business to attend to," Corey answered.

"Okay, no problem, keep in touch and let me know if you have anything else to sell," Jose replied and hand Corey the money, six thousand five hundred.

"Sure, take it easy," John answered as they shook his hand in appreciation and walked out the door.

"I'm so glad I got rid of one burden, thanks John, now all we have to worry about is Lou."

"Stop worrying, he's so scared right now I wouldn't be surprised if he already left Brooklyn."

"Okay, I sure hope you're right. I want to start some kind of business and start a life with Paula. She deserve better than I'm giving her, which is nothing but dreams. I have some more money save up, together with this I should be good."

CHYNA

"It's good you're thinking that way Corey. There's a seminar in Manhattan next week on business start-ups and opportunities. I'll go with you if you're interested."

"Off course I am, we'll go." "Okay, you have to make life what you want it to be, because if you don't, Brooklyn will chew you up and spit you out like bones. Every day one of us dies or goes to jail. Something is not right about this system. I know I'm not an upstanding citizen, but I'm just playing with the cards I was dealt. I will do everything I have to do to survive!"

"That's so true, but do you think as a whole we caused it on ourselves."

"Maybe, but regardless, it is what it is, and nobody seems to have the answer. So as it stands, it's survival of the fittest!"

"Well, I don't believe in evolution. We are civilized human beings with superb intelligence and emotions. We can solve our problems if we really want to, but the ones at the top, the ones in charge want it the way it is. Some kind of class control I think. Consider wild animals, so many of them are close to extinction. We take measures to save them, but who's going to save us if we don't save ourselves?"

CHAPTER 8

Days passed by and there were no signs of retaliation from Lou, which was very comforting to Corey and John. Corey took advantage of the hassle free days by visiting his mother. They went to Church together, where they enjoyed a sermon on "Perilous Times." And then they went to City Island in the Bronx to have dinner, a rite they usually reserved for Easter Sundays. With the way his life is going now, opportunities to socialize and familiarize really are rare and risky. However, because Lou's situation is still looming over his head, 'Paula's plan,' is on the back burner. An evening at Sanctuary also proved to be productive mentally.

CHYNA

"Corey, there's no definite or flawless passage through life. Like I always stress, you are not perfect, no one is, and you will stumble at times. The important thing is to find a way to rise above your circumstance. You are intelligent and strong, not just physically, but mentally. I know you from you were a boy, now you are a man, and a fine one at that. You are the best student I've ever had, and it's an honor to know you. Times are changing rapidly, and so are people. And evil is permeating society at an alarming rate, it's all around us, whether we like it or not. However, the multitude of unproductive distractions that many of us are engaging in daily is causing us to routinely go through each day blindly. You have to stay alert, and by that I mean conscious about everything you do, and everyone you meet.   Hardly anything in our life is happening by chance, someone is pulling strings that are affecting us directly or indirectly. The biggest mistake one can make is to react to events instead of thinking clearly before he acts. Evaluate the people in your life and see who is interested in seeing you elevate. Who wants you in their life if you have nothing else to offer but yourself?   Paula came by to see me. She believes in you and she loves you very much. Don't let her down, because if you do, you will let yourself down. I believe she's that important to you. She is one hundred percent down for you, and that is something money cannot buy." Robert counseled out of deep concern to his protégé. Corey, as usual, became teary eyed.

"I'm trying to do the right thing, and I know the right thing . . . but it's so hard. Sometimes I feel like I'm trapped inside of a body that I can't control, because at times what I don't want to do I find myself doing. Then afterwards I feel so guilty and ashamed. Why is it such a struggle?" Corey asked sincerely.

"Son, I don't have all the answers, but I know for some reasons we tend to act off emotions most of the times instead of off intellect. Maybe it's spiritual, I don't know. I've just met somebody who's opening up my eyes to a whole new world I had little knowledge of, maybe after a few more meetings with him I'll be able to better answer that question for you. Come back and see me tomorrow, you need to be here more often because you're straying from your true self."

"I had planned to, thanks again," he said as they embraced to say goodbye, but then Robert gave him an invitation.

"Why don't you come by the house tonight? The kids are always asking about you, and you know Suzie is crazy about you."

CHYNA

"Well, I don't have anything to do, and I really need a time-out . . . Okay."

Robert Smith's home used to be a second home for Corey, and his wife Suzie was like a second mother to him. She's a stout no-nonsense Christian woman who loves to quote Bible verses. They have twins, a boy and a girl, seven years old. When she got the phone call that Corey was coming over she got overly excited and prepared a place at the dinner table for him, and readied the guess room. She hadn't seen him in about a month, but she treated it like years.

Half an hour later the front door of the Smiths house opened up with a jubilant welcome.

"Oh my . . . look at you, so handsome. God is so good, I pray for you every day," Mrs. Smith gushed as she hugged Corey.

"Thank you, I missed you so much."

"You know our door is open to you anytime, and we love you like our own."

"I know that, it's just that the days are so hectic, and short. Where's Ruth and Rory?"

"Oh, they are fast asleep. They've being playing all day," she answered.

"I'm going to take a shower Corey, you can go ahead and eat without me if you want," Robert said.

"Oh no, I'll wait for you."

"Okay."

"So, have you being reading your bible and going to Church Corey?"

"Occasionally . . . not as often as I would like to, work and school take up all my time."

"All distractions if you ask me, Corey, you have to 'Be sober, be vigilant; because your adversary the devil walks about like a roaring lion, seeking whom he may devour, 1st Peter 5:8.' Evil is everywhere Corey, so you have to 'Put on the whole armor of God, that you may be able to stand against the wiles of the devil. For we do not wrestle against flesh and blood, but against principalities, against powers, against the rulers of the darkness of this age, against spiritual hosts of wickedness in heavenly places.' Ephesians 6:11-12. It's really getting scary to go outside nowadays. You are doomed if you can't recognize the evil around you. My faith reveals it to me Corey, the wickedness we are witnessing now is the sign of the times. If you don't get right with God, your adversary the devil will devour you! You know what I'm talking about, stop playing games and get right, time is running out. I love you, and I want you to be saved!"

"I'm starving . . . ready to eat Corey?" Robert yelled as he entered the dining room. Corey felt rescued, but wouldn't show it out of love and respect for Mrs. Smith.

"You could start without me," he replied.

"It is okay son . . . go ahead and eat, we can continue tomorrow. You're staying here tonight, right?" Mrs. Smith asked.

"Sure, I feel like I'm home, plus I haven't had a good meal in a long time," Corey answered with a smile, and then went to sit around the dinner table.

"Enjoyed the service Corey? She's very zealous about her faith."

"Oh yea, I think I could use a daily dose of that. She has a way of penetrating your soul with her words."

"Yea, she swears she's going to make a Christian out of me, and she just might. There must be an answer to all this wretchedness plaguing the world today. Amidst all this ungodliness her love is steadfast, and her faith makes a very good case. This world is in trouble, and it's getting worse. I'm working on a new charter for our school . . . one that will transform our minds to new heights. We have to not only prepare ourselves for the foreseen, but also for the unforeseen. I need you to start coming back to the school regularly."

"I know, and I'm working my way back. Just one little thing I have to deal with and everything will be back to normal. I got myself into a real sticky situation, but I'm almost out."

"Anything I can do to help, you know all you have to do is ask?"

"I know, but I've got it under control . . . dinner was great. Can't tell the last time I ate like this."

"Well, you know you're welcome anytime. Suzie wouldn't mind if you come by every day, and the kids are crazy about you."

"I know . . . if I could I would. But I promise I will start coming by more often."

"Well I'm beat . . . you know where your room is. I'll see you in the morning."

"Thank you, tell mums I said goodnight."

CHYNA

"Okay, goodnight."

Corey proceeded to take a quick shower and then hit the sack because he was really tired, but thoughts of Mrs. Smiths' sermon, and Robert Smith, his mentor, the tall father figure, no nonsense man of principles permeated his mind. And so his conscience triggered tears as he closed his eyes and drifted off to sleep.

TOO YOUNG TO DIE

CHAPTER 9

The sweet aroma of Jamaican cocoa tea, ackee and saltfish with fried dumplings flowed through the air from room to room until Corey caught a whiff and opened his eyes with a smile. It brought to memory his childhood days in Jamaica when breakfast was his favorite meal of the day. He lay motionless in the bed as he reminisced about Jamaica's mouthwatering foods, its natural beauty and rich culture. His time growing up as a youth going on excursions with his friends to pick mangoes, guineps, plums, apples, guavas, coconuts, ackee, and the many other delicious fruits grown abundantly on that precious island. He's obviously missing home, and begins to delve deeper in his memories, but got interrupted by Robert.

"Good morning Corey, breakfast is ready."

CHYNA

"Okay, I'll be there in a minute," Corey answered and rushed to the bathroom.

It was about 7:00 a.m., and the children were still asleep, but this is the usual wake up time for Mr. and Mrs. Smith. They always began their day with a hearty breakfast. This wasn't new for Corey, just hard. He was out of sync with his culture because he got caught up in a lifestyle that he seemed to be living blindly.

"Good morning," Corey said cheerfully as he took a seat around the table with Mr. and Mrs. Smith, but was reluctant to eat.

"Dig in Corey, we know you don't get to eat like this every day," Robert said.

"True, but I don't usually eat this early."

Suzie and Robert looked at each other and smiled.

"I guess you don't wake up this early either," Suzie said softly.

"No, I guess lately I haven't had much to wake up to," Corey replied softly.

"Well Corey, today can be the start of a new life, if you want it to be," Robert said.

"That is my plan. Today I'm going to a seminar to get help on starting a new business. And I'll propose to Paula. We want to start a family and have a life together."

"That is so sweet, we're so proud of you Corey. Paula will make you so happy. She really loves you," Suzie said with a warm smile.

"I know, and I love her," Corey replied as he took a sip of his cocoa.

"We're here for you, anything you need just let us know," Robert said.

"Thanks, I know," Corey replied as he eased out his chair and stood up, "I have to go, thanks for everything."

Mr. and Mrs. Smith hugged Corey as they fought back tears. They loved him like he was their own son, and they are very proud of him. "He's heading in the right direction." So they thought. Little do they know of the evils he's involved in.

Corey does have good intentions, but his conscience kept reminding him of the reality he faced daily. He fought hard to keep the wretchedness at the back of his mind by entertaining good thoughts and visiting loved ones. But he can't escape. The second he's by himself the mental torture begins and his lament continued.

"If they only knew how I'm failing, would they still feel the same way about me?" He thought to himself.

Corey fought back tears as he drove home while trying to keep his thoughts at bay. His constant struggle to do good is an enigma to him; why is it so hard when it's his will?

As he pulled in his driveway he kept the engine running. He's thinking of going by Paula to patch things up, tell her his plans and hope she'd be happy, but his phone rang.

"Hello."

"Corey, I'm on my way over," John said.

"Okay, I'll see you soon," Corey replied, then killed the engine and went inside to wait for John.

Corey seemed relieved he'll be having company. At least he won't be alone with his thoughts, thoughts that seemed to be causing him too much misery lately. He went and took a shower and put on a nice grey suit.

TOO YOUNG TO DIE

"Today is the start of a new life for me, and I must dress the part," he thought to himself as he looked in a full length mirror in admiration.

The doorbell rang and he went to answer it.

"Wow, it's just a seminar Corey, not a wedding," John said with a smile.

"To you it's a seminar . . . to me it's the start of a new life. I'm taking Paula to dinner later and propose to her, I have to show her I'm serious about us. There has to be more to life than running the streets blindly. We are heading to nowhere fast John. You have to admit that living day to day in uncertainty sometimes makes you feel like you're going crazy. Paula is the end of my uncertainty, she's my future, and I'm ready to take that journey with her."

"Great speech . . . and I wish you all the best. Let's go make it happen," John replied with enthusiasm.

CHÝNA

CHAPTER 10

The sight of the Hell Gate Bridge gave Corey and John an eerie feeling as they drove behind a motorcade of black limousines across the Triborough Bridge towards Wards Island, the location of the seminar. The fog and overcast sky didn't ease the ghoulish feelings they are beginning to have. They even joked that they may be on their way to some kind of a macabre cult event.

As they parked amongst the multitude of vehicles and noticed the hundreds of people entering through a gate, to the wide open park like area where the seminar is taking place, there feeling of angst disappeared.

"Wow, there must be thousands of people here," John said excitedly.

"I know, as we were coming over the bridge I was getting second thoughts."

"Wait, isn't that Amy?" John asked pointing ahead towards the gate.

"It sure is. What's she doing here?"

"Well, let's go find out."

They hurried towards her and noticed she had on a badge of some sort, and handing out pamphlets.

"Corey, you miss me!" Amy blurted out in excitement as she saw him coming towards her.

"Sure . . . you're working?"

"No silly. I'm volunteering, a favor for my father, he's one of the speakers here today. Here," Amy said as she took her father's ring off her finger and slipped it on Max's, "this will get you special privileges while you're here."

"Really . . . I don't know," Corey replied thinking of giving back the ring and John intervened.

CHYNA

"Don't be stupid Corey, we need any advantage we can get . . . you see how much people in this place. Come on, they're about to begin," John said.

"Thanks Amy, I'll see you later."

"Okay, I'll find you when I'm free," she replied with a smile.

"Wow, you sure got her wrapped around your finger, she's not even mad at you for dissing her the other day," John said.

The first speaker to the podium was the judge, Amy's father, a very stout man, garbed in his judicial robe striking an imposing figure.

"I extend to you all our most sincere gratitude for your presence on behalf of my colleagues whom you'll all meet shortly. This meeting will be unlike any you've ever attended before. You are here seeking opportunity and we are here to give it to you, but not just opportunity. We will give you power beyond your wildest imaginations, the kind of power that will make you operate above the law and accumulate fame and riches you've only dreamed of before. Simply put, we are here to make your dreams come true, and the price to you is simple. . . ." Suddenly there was a loud scream coming from the crowd of people standing next to Corey and John.

"Argh!" John blurted out as he grabbed on to Corey while falling to the ground. He had a knife stuck in his back which blood was gushing from. The crowd scrambled as Corey looked up to see Lou standing in front of him smiling, and his hands covered with blood.

Frozen, and staring in disbelief, everyone and everything seemed to be moving in slow motion as Corey tried to make sense of what's going on.

"Corey!" Amy blurted out, and awoke him from his trance, "you okay?"

"You need to get out of here, now!" Corey yelled and pushed Amy to the side as he moved swiftly towards Lou.

"Really, you think you stand a chance?" Lou asked as a group of people quickly stepped between them in his defense.

Corey was shocked to see who his enemies were. Most of them he knew, some he even thought were his friends. Yvonne Fields was amongst them, so were Ron and the rest of his gambling buddies. Now he's beginning to get an idea about the club everyone's being trying to get him to join. With John lying dead at his feet he felt alone, crushed, and defeated.

"You should leave now, the cops will be here any minute," Yvonne said.

Corey looked at Amy, but she turned away as her father, the judge, made his way towards them.

"You don't have to run," he said with his right arm stretched out to Corey, "join us."

Corey, still in a fighting stance, and speechless, is contemplating whether to run or fight.

"I'd rather go to prison," Corey yelled as he attacked Lou with a flurry of kicks and karate chops that sent him bloodied to the ground. The loud piercing sounds of police sirens came screeching towards them didn't prevent Lou's friends from attacking Corey. But with vengeance on his mind and the rage of a mad bull he displayed fighting skills that rendered them powerless and defeated. He looked around for one friendly face in Amy, but she kept walking away with her father.

"*Only one thing to do, run for my life,*" he thought, and that he did.

TOO YOUNG TO DIE

Before the police reached the scene, Corey disappeared and hid in his car and watched from a distant. The police didn't take any information or wrote a report, they just laughed and talked with Amy's father, Lou, Yvonne, and Ron, while John lay on the ground dead.

"They really operate above the law," Corey thought, then slowly drove away.

"That Corey is special, we need to get him to join us at whatever cost. He could be a great asset to us, get him!" The judge ordered.

"We've being trying," Ron answered, "we might have to force him."

"You know we don't care, do whatever you have to, our time is limited."

"Yes sir," Ron said as he looked at Lou and the other goons.

The judge walked off with his arm around Amy.

"Come on Sweetie, you have a lot of explaining to do."

"I know daddy, he's just too stubborn," she replied sheepishly.

CHYNA

Corey is now speeding across the bridge entering Queens, all the while wondering if they had let him leave. They seemed to have the power to keep him on the island, and they didn't even pursue him.

"Why not?" he's wondering, *"and, am I wanted for murder now, why did Amy deserted me, how does Yvonne fit into this group? All these questions and no answers,"* he's thinking to himself as he tried to process the evil that he had just witness. As Corey raced to get home, so was his heart and mind racing to control his equilibrium and figure out a resolve. It feels like every bad decision he had ever made in his life had teamed up and came crashing down on him. This burden feels unbearable, but he knows giving in is a matter of life or death. As he reached home he rushed into his bedroom and grabbed his passport and all the cash he had handy. And as he was about to leave he noticed the fake license plate hanging behind his door with the words: 'Too Young To Die,' he grabbed it, bagged it, and high-tailed it toward Paula's house.

"Whatever I do and wherever I go from now on she has to be with me. I just hope she's not still mad at me, I wonder if I should tell her what's happening to me, should I get her involved, it's not fair to her," he thought to himself as he parked across the street from her house.

TOO YOUNG TO DIE

He exited his car and looked around carefully to make sure he's not walking into a trap. Everything seemed okay, so he walked up to her door and rang the doorbell several times but got no answer. He felt disappointed, thinking that she's just ignoring him because she's mad at him. He was right. She was standing behind the door crying profusely, and contemplating, while fighting not to compromise her virtues. He had insulted her intelligence, betrayed her trust and her love. Now in this time of pain and desperation she's the only one that can give him some relief and hope. Her love is the only remedy for this dreadful affliction he's experiencing. But she doesn't know the pain he's feeling right now. And he doesn't know the pain she's feeling either.

Disheartened and desperate, Corey hobbled back to his car with tears in his eyes. Paula watched him, still crying and fighting the urge to open the door, but lost all her strength and dropped to the floor. And then with a burst of energy she jumped to her feet, opened the door and ran out screaming his name.

"Corey! Corey! Corey!" She yelled, but it was too late, he had driven off lonely, into the turmoil of the uncertain world they both dread with disgust. Realizing that she too might be facing this uncertain world alone, she went back inside and cried herself to sleep.

CHÝNA

CHAPTER 11

Jamaica: land of wood and water, and the birthplace of sweet reggae music. Lush green rainforests, emerald mountains, natural mineral springs, winding rivers, cascades, coral reefs, groves of coconut palms, sugar plantations, and long beautiful stretches of white sandy beaches are visible as Corey gazed through the window while the plane anticipated landing at Sangster International Airport in Montego Bay. Childhood memories overwhelmed him and a tinge of guilt spurred a sense of shame. *"I should have being coming back more often, how will I face the people who nurtured me as a child. Will they welcome me with open arms*?" He wondered. But he knew Jamaica is a forgiving place, and its people are happy go lucky with smiles as big as their hearts. Sit and talk with a Jamaican and all your worries will seem to disappear. No problem, cool runnings, irie, good friend betta dan pocket money, blessings, respect, and every ting criss, are just some of the slangs and phrases that dominate their conversations. Those are feel good words that put you at ease and compel you to smile even if you don't have a reason to.

It's about five in the evening, and Corey is bubbling with excitement as he made his way out of the airport amongst equally excited tourists. He noticed a woman scolding her unruly teenage son who was arguing with her, and a rasta man stepped in to help.

"Why do you argue with your mom, don't you know she loves you and everything she does and says to you will always be in your best interest. Never argue with her, she knows you more than you know yourself, and she probably experienced everything you already had and will. She's older and wiser than you, and she's trying to mold you into a real man by building your character and teach you the values you need to know to survive and thrive in this world," he said to the teenager who listened attentively.

"Need a taxi brethren?" the rasta man asked smoothly as he noticed Corey walking by, "I know every part of this island, and everyone in it."

"Really, then you must know Junior," Corey replied with just a hint of his Jamaican accent, and the Rasta man burst out in laughter.

"The man is a Jamaican . . . nuff respect. Tell me which parish him live, and I will find him fe you. Let me get that bag for you brethren," he replied.

"Thanks, but it's cool. I'll carry it. Where's your car?"

"Just follow me boss man, no problem."

Corey followed him across the street to his car, a white Toyota Corolla.

"Nice ride, how far is St. Ann from here?"

"Depends how fast you want to get there . . . anywhere from half an hour to a week, oh . . . and the money. You know say time is money."

"Okay, by the way, I'm Corey."

"My name is Savant, because me wise, but you can call me Ras."

"Cool, Savant it is, I want to go to Ochi, but no rush, just get me there safely."

"No problem . . . so this Junior is he a relative or a friend?"

"I was just kidding, there's no Junior. I just miss Jamaica and want to come relax for a while."

"How long the man a stay?"

"I don't know yet, I have to make some calls first before I decide."

"If you need a driver you can hire me, I'm very reasonable, here, keep my card with you in case."

"Okay, but I know my way around so I might just get a rental. Stop! Pull over by that fruit stand!" Corey yelled.

"Okay, but talk like a Jamaican, or them will charge you like a tourist."

Be warned, that driving down a Jamaican street at any given time, the sweet aroma of mouthwatering jerk chicken, the sight and scent of exotic tropical fruits, or even the sweet sound of reggae beats will entice you to make a pit stop. Corey couldn't resist as his mouth salivates at the sight of the variety of fruits that he enjoyed as a child growing up in Jamaica. He took a bag and filled it with two of each fruit, then he asked for a freshly cut water coconut. After he finished he pulled out his wallet to pay, but the man refused his money.

"It's on the house, enjoy your stay here in Jamaica," the man said.

"It's okay, I want to pay," Corey insisted, but the man kept nodding his head no.

"Come on star, don't insult the man, let's go," Savant said and took the bag of fruits from Corey.

"Thank you," Corey finally said and followed Savant back to the car.

Corey, perplexed, sit silently in the car as Savant sped off.

"Nobody have to tell me twice to keep my money, Corey, that man likes you. You know why?"

"My good looks."

"Wrong, you didn't notice the tattoo pon him hand?"

TOO YOUNG TO DIE

Before Corey could respond a police car sped up behind them with the sirens blaring.

"What now?" Savant said in disgust as he pulled over.

"Police don't like rasta and rasta don't like police, this is going to be interesting," Corey is thinking to himself.

The officer walked over to the car looking real serious.

"Seems like you in a real hurry dread. You don't know say speed kills?" The officer asked looking at Savant and Corey.

"Sorry Officer, I didn't realize I was speeding," Savant replied softly.

"Sorry can't help me, looks like I'm going to have to write you a big fat ticket. At a matter of fact, both of you step out of the car, I think I smell weed."

"No officer, we weren't smoking," Savant pleaded as he opened the car door. Corey remained silent, and obedient. He opened the door and stepped out, but to his surprise, the officer quickly backed away from him.

"Sorry dread, just gwaan, and stop the speeding," the officer said and went back into his car in a hurry, and then he made a quick u turn and sped off.

CHYNA

"Now I'm really confused," Corey said, "people are acting strange. What's going on?"

"You blind . . . or you dumb?" Savant asked sternly, "you no see the policeman have the same tattoo like the man at the fruit stand?"

"So?" Corey asked . . . still confused.

"Look at the ring pon you finger man, the emblem on it is the same picture pon them tattoos. I bet you don't even know what it means, right?"

"No, this ring is not even mines. I didn't even realize I still have it on. I'm at war with them . . . Shit! They must think I'm a member of their club. I can't believe their tentacles reached all the way down here."

"It's global, and it's as evil as evil can get. I didn't want to say anything to you, because we were just doing business. I know a little something about them."

"Okay, I can't believe this . . . I'm trapped!"

"Yeah, you are. And so are a lot of people, but they can't see it unless they step out of the box and look in from the outside at what's going on. I can see it because I was in that same box and decided to step out of it."

TOO YOUNG TO DIE

"You're confusing me Savant, even your flip flopping accent . . . and you're supposed to be wise."

"Okay, didn't mean to. I was in America, lived there for about fifteen years, but moved back here after I finished college, that damned student loan was too much of a burden. Their outdated school system felt more like indoctrination than education. And most people like us don't benefit from their system. The average person work hard all their life and have to mandatorily pay into social security, but how many of us live to see retirement, and how many of us will lose those benefits because of our status. And seeing how easy it was for people to get caught up in crime, drugs, and alcohol was a risk I wasn't willing to take. Believe me, if I didn't make a conscious effort to resist peer pressure when I was younger I would've become a victim, and sadly, society would've branded me a criminal. Have a smoke, take a drink, try this, try that . . . Just one try and you could be hooked for life and become a slave to their evil ways. Say no and you become an outcast, a misfit nobody wants to be around. Don't get me wrong, there are some good people out there, but you have to make a conscious effort to find them. To be cool and hip you have to be socially correct, usually doing some bad things. But it's all a trap, designed by a real sophisticated network of evil men and women. That ring you're wearing represents that society. Some call it a secret society, but it's not all secret, only their agenda is. They're on a universal mission to use, and then drag mankind into the pits of hell,   and they're starting with the children. Am I sounding crazy? Because that's the response I get whenever I start talking about this."

"No Savant, you're making a lot of sense, now I know why you have that name."

"They'll entice you with promises of fame and success, and if you refuse they'll cast a line with the right bait, until you bite. Bite . . . and you will most likely get hooked. Your weakness is the bait that they will use, whether it being women, money, drugs, whatever! How many times have they thrown their line your way . . . did you bite, and what does it profit a man to gain the whole world but loses his own soul?"

"I think we all bite sometimes, but not everybody got hooked. But I am beginning to see inside that box you talked about . . . from the outside, and it makes a lot of sense to me. A lot of people I love are in that box."

"Not because they are in the box means they are hooked. You can be in the box unhooked, but still in danger, because they never stop throwing lines with different baits hoping you will bite. And if you don't bite, they will instill fear in you. Once you get the knowledge of their operation and goal you have a responsibility to let others know and help them to resist the temptations."

"Where did you get all this knowledge, from the good old ganja? They said it was first discovered growing out of The Great King Solomon's grave."

"I went to school just like you, but I watched and I learned. Whenever I see wicked men indulging in their folly I observed and see the consequences and wraths that they produced. We should all be living good with each other and enjoy life to the fullest. The Creator gives us everything to enjoy, but some abuse it, even kill to have more than the next man. What are we fighting each other for? We must leave everything behind when our time here is up. Jamaica is not perfect, but I would rather live here amongst my people and enjoy the beautiful sunshine and best food inna the world. Jamaica to the fullest, one love we a deal with."

"No place like Jamaica, a yah so nice," Corey said.

"There was a man who one day went to the zoo and saw a crowd of people gathered by a monkey's pen. They were watching the monkey putting on a spectacular show, so he too got mesmerized as he watched and enjoyed. It became a ritual for him, as he would go by the zoo every Sunday just to be in that crowd of happy people watching that monkey doing his thing.

One Sunday as the man walked towards the monkey's pen he noticed there was no crowd, and when he reached the pen he saw workers cleaning and closing the pen. He asked one worker what happened, and the worker told him that the monkey had died. He became sad and as he walked off slowly he noticed others were grieving the monkey's death also. Obviously the monkey was greatly missed, and many people were sad.

Before the man left the zoo he was struck with an idea, so he went to find the zoo keeper. 'That monkey was your best attraction, and many people, including me, were happy watching him do his tricks. What if I can dress up as a monkey and go in the same pen and do some of those tricks, would you hire me?' He asked. 'I can't pay you much, and you will do it at your own risk,' the zoo keeper answered. 'No problem, the man said, and went home joyfully to work on his costume. The next Sunday he went to the zoo elated and ready to pretend to be a monkey, and as the crowd gathered he begins to do back-flips and relished in the applause. He sensed the crowd wanted more, so he climbed and hang on to the rope over his pen and begins to swing; the applause got louder, and the crowd demanded more. *'What can I do to top that?'* he thought, asking himself. And then he noticed the rope he was swinging from stretched all the way over to the lions' den.

And so he begins to do the unthinkable, swinging towards the lions' den; and the crowd stared silently in awe. He dangled from the rope over the lions' den teasing the lions that were jumping up and biting at his feet. It was great entertainment, but very risky, and the crowd was enjoying it, but at the same time biting their nails. Suddenly the monkey slipped from the rope and fell into the lions' den, and the crowd screamed and cried out for help as they tossed anything they could to scare off the lions. But the lions continued to move in for the kill as the monkey backed into a corner. The monkey/man, scared to death, grabbed the face of his mask and begins to rip it off while shouting: 'I'm not a real monkey, I'm a man!' The lions rushed him and whispered: 'Shut up, we're not real lions either. You're going to mess it up for all of us.'

Corey burst out in laughter, "that was really funny," he chuckled.

"Yeah, but it's not just a joke, there are multiple morals to the story: (1) Appearances are deceptive, (2) It

CHYNA

is difficult to change the inborn characteristic of a person, and the most important one, (3) Everyone wears a mask, everybody have something to hide, and no one wants you to know everything about them, only what they want you to know. Always remember that. I believe that was one of Aesop's fables, I read it on a wall in someone's office a long time ago, and I never forget it. I told it to you hoping it will resonate in some way while you're here and meeting new people, and even whenever you go back to America."

"I get it, that story is like a gold mine, full of nuggets, we're almost in Ochi, how much do I owe you?"

"Sixty dollars . . . American of course, you seem like a good man Corey, wish you was staying in Mo-bay. I would check you every day," Savant said as he pulled up in front of the hotel.

"Thanks, I'll call you before I leave, maybe we could have a drink."

"That would be great, be careful out here. Nice as Jamaica is, evil still lurks. You can still pretend to be one of them by keep wearing that ring, but why keep your hand inna the lion mouth when you know him can bite it off."

TOO YOUNG TO DIE

"You're right, I'll take it off. Here's a hundred, you deserve more, but I don't want to overpay you."

"Ahh . . . you're funny. Thanks. I wish you all the best Corey, call me if I can help you with anything, and I mean anything."

"I will . . . thanks again," Corey said as he walked off into the lobby of The Jamaica Grande. Savant waited until he was at the desk then drove off back to Montego Bay.

A short, but very edifying journey had come to an end, but one that might be a catalyst to start a revolution with monumental ramifications. Savant has opened Corey's mind to a world he was a part of, but never perceived. How serious did he take it, and is he willing to take action against such an organization. Before, he was driven by his will to stay alive. "Too young to die," was the words he used to remind himself daily to meet the challenges of his community.

Now the stakes are higher . . . if what Savant said is all true, then the whole world is at stake, and is he interested in taking on this grand symbolic struggle.

"I am but one man, on the run with no resources but my will to survive. How can I stand up to something so

bigger and powerful than I had ever imagined. Me against the world it feels like, but somehow I'm not afraid. Should I be? Why didn't they just kill me when they had the chance? There must be more to this, something I'm missing, something probably far beyond the scope of Savant's knowledge."

Corey was really tired, but deep in thoughts, lying on the bed with his eyes closed and hoping that sleep would come to rescue him.

Elsewhere in America, far across the ocean, somewhere in Brooklyn in a dungeon like basement, a clandestine meeting convenes. And Corey Young is the reason. Amy's father, The Judge, Lou, Ron, Yvonne, and a host of ghoulish looking characters cloaked in black hoodies chants in a cryptic language. A door opened and the dungeon becomes silent as every shadow turned to face what seemed to be their leader. Shrouded in a black robe with a hoodie over his head, his face was not visible.

And he speaks with a deep bellowing voice. "Comrades, I see we have a problem. The target has fled from us, how could that be? I was promised him as a trophy. Now you're planning to kill him. The plan was to strategically entice him with his weaknesses: money and sex, since he detests drugs and alcohol. I understood he took both from you, but somehow you couldn't turn him. He is but a mere man, born of the flesh with the same lustful desires like everyone else. Maybe you didn't give him enough. Whilst he's still walking in limbo, with no God, we can still win him over. Kill him now, and we'll only add another soul. Look at the big picture, win him over, and with his talents we can gain a city, or even a nation. He can be an asset to us. I want him, find a way to his heart, you know his weaknesses, feed it! And if that doesn't work, instill fear in him. Break him! Whatever it takes . . . get him!" The bellowing sound echoed as he turned around and disappeared through the doors he had entered from, and then his ghoulish comrades began mumbling amongst themselves.

How do you defeat a man that has no fear? A diabolical scheme to get Corey seemed to be brewing, and this wasn't the first time. Seems like Corey's relationship with Amy, Danny's death, his gambling habit, and his escapade with Ron, was all a diabolical scheme to lure him into a sinisterly web of everlasting turmoil to gain his soul. What a price for man to pay, especially when he has no knowledge and everything seemed coincidental. Fair to say, without knowledge one is at the mercy of his adversary. And if this is true, then Danny Fields might have been collateral damage, and now his wife is in bed with the devil. They have their orders, and at any cost they must succeed.

CHAPTER 12

Crack of dawn and the cool island breeze gushed through the open windows caressing Corey's face while the gentle waves of the Caribbean Sea whispered a sweet lullaby. Well rested and rejuvenated, mentally and physically, he stretched and smiled as he climbed out of bed. He picked up a menu and stepped out to the patio to face the rising sun.

CHYNA

"Ahhh," He exhaled with outstretched arms, feeling relieved and relaxed. He then sit on a lounge chair and examined the menu.

"A good breakfast is the best way to start the day," he thought, reminiscing of his childhood days.

As he enjoyed his breakfast on the patio the sweet melodies of Bob Marley singing, 'everything's gonna be alright,' reverberated through the air and put a warm smile on his face.

"I could sit here forever," he said to himself, absorbing the cool breeze, the warm sun, and beautiful music as he watched couples strolling hand in hand along the beach. All his troubles seemed to be forgotten, even Paula, his true love, seemed to be out of his mind.

"Jamaica will do this to you, everyone and everything seemed to move at a relaxed pace. I believe because the breeze smells so fresh, the fruits are so luscious, the food so succulent, and the beautiful beaches. Even the sun feels good, not as harsh as in Florida or New York. I couldn't sit outside this long in Florida? I would be sweating and dehydrating so fast I would need medical

attention. *This is where home should be,*" he's thinking to himself.

How easy it is for one to get lost in a moment, wallowing in his state of mind, and forgetting there's a purpose for his existence. It's okay to take a break sometimes, but regain your composure and get back into the saddle. There's a race to run, and how we run it will determine our fate, and maybe the fate of countless others. Our actions have implications that will affect not only us, but others too, now and in the future.

Corey started out as a pawn, but now he has become the king. And if captured it is game over. His present state of mind is making him vulnerable, even with the knowledge Savant had bequeathed him, he doesn't realize the army mobilizing against him.

As the days unfold Corey put pen to paper writing poems to past the time and forget his troubles back in America. He took strolls on the beach, walks in the country side, and lounges at night in the hotel's café. He seemed to have given up on that life back in America, and is embarking on a new one that seemed more fitting for a much older man. He is only twenty six, vigorous and ambitious . . . so, how long can he keep this up?

CHYNA

It's a cool night in the café, and Corey is at a table by himself enjoying a Pina colada. A songstress is singing the blues while staring at him intensely, and he seemed mesmerized.

"I put a spell on you," she croons, and the words seemed to have penetrated his heart. He leaned back into his chair, salivating in lust, as the beautiful songstress dressed in a red satin dress serenades the crowd. But Corey took it personal.

At the end of her number she walked over to the bar, and Corey followed.

"Hi, I'm Corey, can I buy you a drink?" He asked smoothly.

"No need, it's all inclusive . . . but thank you anyway," she replied with a smile.

"Wow, see the effect you have on me. I feel like a total idiot."

"That's not a good effect, maybe you should stay away from me," she said wryly.

"Wrong choice of words . . . I meant you give me butterflies."

"How interesting, was it my voice, or my eyes?" She asked seductively, and he bent over and whispered softly in her ear.

"A combination of both . . . I would love to dance with you before the night is over."

His lips against her ear sent chills up her spine and she quivered sensually. She gulped nervously as she tried to utter a response.

"Shhh . . . sure, but I sing better than I dance. You'll have to lead me . . . and I'm not a good follower," she purred.

"Don't worry I'm a good leader, how about the next song?" Corey asked confidently.

"I don't know if I'm ready, my legs feel weak," she said while taking a sip of her drink.

"That's the effect I have on you?" He asked amusedly.

"Don't flatter yourself," she said with a wide smile, "I was on my feet all night entertaining you, remember?"

"Then I'll accept a raincheck, can we just sit by my table and talk some more?"

"Sure, as long as I'm off my feet."

They walked over to the table and Corey pulled a chair for her to sit.

"Very impressive, I thought chivalry was dead," she said with a twinkle in her eyes.

"Not dead, just scarce. Feminism is mostly responsible for that."

"Really, I guess submission have its benefits then."

"I guess, we'll just have to wait and see. You live here?"

"No, vacationing. But tonight is just a warm up for my upcoming tour next week in New York."

"Oh, so you're a real singer?"

"How did you guess?" She asked with a grin.

"Just kidding, you sing beautifully. You had me hypnotized, if the song didn't end I would still be sitting with my jaws hanging and my mind wondering."

"So, where was your mind while I was singing?"

"I can't tell you, I'd be embarrassed."

"But I bet you can show me, right?"

"I could if you let me."

"Say I agree . . . I will have to go back to your hotel room, right?"

"Yeah."

"Typical male chauvinist, I am one of those millennium chicks . . . I'm a shot caller, not a man follower! Follow me enough and I might just let you . . ." she said boldly while handing him a brochure and then stepped off.

Corey was dumbfounded, *"What just happened*?" He seemed to be asking himself, staring at her as she stormed out of the café. He slowly looked around, feeling embarrassed, but he had no spectators. He then looked at the brochure and noticed she had scribbled her room number down with a note, "I want you to show me," it reads.

Excited . . . he hurried out after her.

Sexual appetite is like dynamite. Powerful and filled with suspense, and the explosion can be catastrophic. Corey is reacting to his lustful desires, blindly following the trail left by the songstress, a woman he had just met and knows nothing about.

CHYNA

As he turned a corner and neared her room he could see her walking in and leaving the door open. He entered and closed the door behind him, and to his surprise she was already half naked. Clothes and shoes on the floor, and clad only in her bra and panty, *"she looks amazing,"* he thought to himself.

"Why the scene?" He asked bemused.

"I have a reputation to protect," she said softly with a smile, "and I believe you have something to show me."

"I do," he whispered softly and engulfed her in his arms. Passionately they engaged fulfilling their lust, and enjoying each other as the night whisked by leaving them wanting. The night didn't seemed long enough, but as dawn broke she scurried to get dress, and Corey wanted more. As she brushed her hair he tried to undress her and she allowed him, then he laid her on the bed . . . but suddenly she pushed him off.

"Sorry, I have to catch a plane back to the States in about two hours," she explained. A great tease she was.

"Really, now you're telling me," he replied, and jumped up to hug her.

TOO YOUNG TO DIE

"I'm sorry, I should have told you, but you gave me butterflies," she said with a wide smile.

"Can you tell me your name so I can find you?"

They both burst out in laughter, their time together had flew by so fast but created so much pleasure.

"Sherene Parker, but you should forget about me, I'm no good for you," she said with tears trickling from her eyes.

"What are you talking about? I can't remember ever feeling like this. We must see each other again," he said softly.

"You have no idea who I am . . . I made a mistake, I'm sorry but I have to go Corey," she said and kissed him goodbye.

"See you soon . . . Sherene," he replied as she walked out the door, and maybe his life.

America had become a distant memory, now Sherene is giving him reasons to entertain fresh new thoughts that could pull him back into a place where misery abounds. He's putting up a good fight, but the feelings and images of last night are too fresh in his mind, and too powerful to defeat, even when memories of Paula began creeping in, so he's really struggling to separate them.

He went back into bed and closed his eyes, hoping that sleep would rescue him from his mental torture, a trick he had tried before, but that turned out to be just a temporary fix.

TOO YOUNG TO DIE

CHAPTER 13

The afternoon sun was hot, but the cool Caribbean breeze neutralized its effect. Corey rolled over on the plush king size bed blurting out a long sigh of relief. And then he reached for a folder and began reading out loud one of the poems he had written:

CHYNA

Missing You

Even though we are miles apart,

You're always in my heart,

Out of sight out of mind,

Nonsense . . . I declined.

Longing makes the heart grows fonder,

True, but I'd rather have you closer,

To kiss, hug, and hold you when I want,

Because right now I miss you and I can't.

This pain is driving me crazy,

All I'm feeling is misery.

I have to find my way back to you,

No matter what circumstance may brew.

To live without you,

I just cannot do.

TOO YOUNG TO DIE

As he finished reading, an obvious feeling of despair overwhelmed him. Tears filled his eyes as he cringed with emotional pain. What or who is causing this writhing? Couldn't be Sherene; that poem was written before last night. Last night may have awoken his conscience and allowed Paula to creep in and wreak havoc on his state of mind. And reading the poem must have made him realized she deserved to be by his side. Guilt might be riding him . . . having this much fun by himself, infidelity, and ignoring his true feelings must have made him feel shameful and despicable.

One cannot run away from himself, maybe from a place, or a person, or a circumstance . . . but never from himself. One cannot put aside his mind and go his separate way! Our mind is what makes us aware we are alive, perceive the world we're in, and have feelings and emotions. It is the faculty by which we recognized the distinction between right and wrong regarding our conduct. It ignites guilt or hostility, compassion or understanding. In our mind, we contemplate and compromise virtue, indignities, and corruption.

Corey is obviously struggling within himself, and the pain is manifesting his humanity. He appeared emotionally drained and physically weak, but mustered up enough strength to call and book a flight back to America. Then he called Savant.

"Greetings," Savant answered jubilantly.

"Brethren, I need a ride to the airport now."

"What time?"

"4:00 p.m. flight."

"No problem, I'll leave now."

"Okay, great. I'll see you soon."

"Irie," Savant replied.

And at the same time, way across the Atlantic in America, Paula Smart visits Sanctuary in search of Corey. Seemed time had healed the wound Corey had caused her. It's hard to forgive someone who break your heart, but it's even harder to forget someone who was once your everything. She's missing her man and decided it's time to forgive him and patch things up. However, Corey is nowhere to be found; no one had a clue to where he was, not even Robert Smith. He noticed her from his office, and she looked distraught and lonesome, so he sent for her.

TOO YOUNG TO DIE

She entered his office optimistic, but quickly became disappointed when she learned Robert was in the dark just as much as she was.

"I'm sorry Paula, he seemed fine the last time I saw him. At a matter of fact, he was ecstatic, because he was going to ask you to marry him. But from the look of things it looked like he never did," Robert said looking perplexed.

"No, he came by to see me but I never let him in. I was still hurting from his betrayal . . . but I can't stop thinking about him. He means everything to me, and I want to tell him. But now it might be too late," she said timidly.

"I wouldn't worry too much, he probably needed some time alone . . . he'll come around, he always do."

"I think he's in some kind of trouble, I can feel it."

"If he is, he can take care of himself. He's the strongest kid I've ever known."

"He is strong . . . I just hope he's alright. Later I'll go by his house."

"And tell him to come see me, it's very important."
"Okay, I will if I see him," she said as she hugged Robert goodbye.

CHYNA

Savant was excited to see Corey again, not just because of business, but because Corey was receptive to his intellectual consultation on their first meet. And he felt he was fulfilling a purpose, a purpose that could have monumental implications on the world. Savant is a man of conviction, and he recognized that Corey was on the same battlefield that he had deserted years ago. Now that Corey is about to reenter that battlefield, he felt if he could equip him with the necessary knowledge, Corey could fight, and probably win the battle that he had ran away from years ago. As he neared the hotel he called Corey to inform him, and Corey was ready and waiting.

"Oh, it is good to see you again my friend," Savant said jubilantly as he jumped out of the car and hugged Corey.

"It is good to see you too, wish it was under different circumstances, but I have to rush back to the States."

"No problem, I hope it's nothing bad."

"Not really, just have some unfinished business I think I should clear up," Corey replied.

"Okay, let's roll if you're ready."

"Let's roll . . . Jamaica is so beautiful, I can hardly wait to come back."

"It is. I'm surprised you're leaving so soon. Is it a woman?"

"Why, is it obvious?

"No, I'm just curious. A man might look as strong as a bull, but without self-control he is just as weak as a newborn, especially when it comes to women. Remember Sampson and Delilah, they should be a lesson to every man today, but we still make the same mistake. Sampson had all that power, and because of the kratches he revealed the secret of his power to Delilah. Even in that event you can see that knowledge is really power, and even the kratches have power."

"Why did you become a taxi driver, you should have become a teacher," Corey replied sternly.

"Then I wouldn't meet interesting people like you Corey, there's a reason we meet you know. This didn't happen by chance."

"I guess I'm lucky."

"Or blessed, you know the difference?"
"I'm sure you're going to tell me," Corey answered smiling.

CHYNA

"Which addiction do you think is worse: smoking, alcohol, sex, drugs, or gambling?"

"I would say drugs," Corey answered.

"I would say they are all the same, even though they manifest different debilitating physical signs. Look at the mental consequence; they all lead to the same slavish dependence. The effects don't start from outside in, but inside out. Your first taste is satisfying, and then you develop a craving and do all you can to satisfy that crave. You will neglect everything and everyone important to you just to fulfill that crave. And before you know it you've become a slave to that weakness. My point is . . . the battle is within. Win the battle inside first and then you can take on the one outside . . . *'But I see another law in my members, warring against the law of my mind, and bringing me into captivity to the law of sin which is in my members'* . . .," Romans 7:23-25," Savant said in a preachy manner.

"What are you talking about?" Corey asked bemused.

"Pay attention, your life depends on it, and when I quote from the Bible I hope you don't get offended. Even if a person is not a Christian, or from another religious sect, they should be open to knowledge. When someone tell you something, or you read something that seem like a mystery, or you don't understand it, you should never dismiss it, but do some digging or research to find out for yourself if it's the truth. A person's addiction is always their biggest weakness, and is a detriment to his or her survival. Satan is evil incarnate, he has to work through people who will cooperate with him for whatever reason. Imagine America as a new world you are about to enter and the government and its people are out to get you. But there are laws that protect you. Even if they break those laws they still can't harm you. Only if you yourself break those laws will you give them the power to harm you. Now, this is the reality: you are going back into a world where the true rulers are out to get you, but the only way they can get you is if you break the law of God which protects you. When one commits a sin he gives the ruler of this world, Satan, an invitation to come into his life and wreak havoc. *'For we do not wrestle against flesh and blood, but against principalities, against powers, against the rulers of the darkness of this age . . . '* Ephesians 6:12. Yes Corey, you are living in their world . . . *'but greater is He that is in you than he that is in this world.'* 1st John 4:4. The majority of us spend our days reacting to events, so it's easy for us to fall into a trap. We must learn to be proactive, make things happen instead of responding to what happen . . . Be a force . . . don't be enforced!"

CHYNA

"Man, you have my head spinning. When I think about it, everything you're saying makes sense. But I don't know where to start."

"You are stronger than you know, because you have a spirit within you that they cannot defeat. Have faith, and believe that you have the power within. Here, I brought this for you," Savant said and handed Corey a Bible.

"A Bible, thanks, I didn't know you read the Bible."

"Everybody reads the Bible, even if they do it inside their closet. Where you think I really get my wisdom from, ganja?" Savant replied and they burst out in laughter, "remember when we were growing up here in Jamaica it was mandatory for us to go to church and Sunday school. Many of us never grasp the real deep meaning of what we were supposed to be learning. But we have to admit that the church did give us a strong foundation of how to be a good person. We learned morals, how to love and be compassionate one to another, and respect all life. America is a great country, but with all its freedoms and tolerance it's citizens have to pay a hefty price, and sometimes that is their soul. I don't want to make that sacrifice, and that's why I'm here in Jamaica. We are not perfect, but because we don't have to cater for so much different types of people, and dabble with the many different cultures, we have less stress. I am stress free, and that's a good feeling."

"Here we are again, at the end of another seminar," Corey said while smiling, "I'm going to miss you brethren, and I do appreciate your wisdom."

"I'll be with you in spirit; don't let them frighten

you . . . you know who I'm talking about, right?" Savant asked while shaking his hand goodbye.

"Yes, I know. Thanks again, I'll be back soon and we'll have that drink."

"Cool, I'll be waiting," Savant replied waving goodbye as Corey heads inside the airport.

Corey strides in confidence, equipped with a new knowledge of his adversaries; but is he going back to fight a war, or is he going back to fetch the love of his life? Whatever the reason, Corey seem confident. Whether or not one believes the Bible is the infallible truth of The Creator, there is knowledge in it, and knowledge is power, that we can all admit. Who doesn't want to have power, be a conqueror, and overcome evil? . . . I'm just saying.

CHYNA

CHAPTER 14

7:30 pm, close to dusk, and as the plane prepared for landing Corey reminisced about the first time he had touched down in America. But now the anticipations are different, the expectations are different, and so are his reasons. He's not that delicate, gullible and innocent boy anymore. He's now a man, vigorous, skeptical, and has a purpose.

TOO YOUNG TO DIE

The picturesque view from above as the plane anticipated landing was still beautiful. But his memories had reaffirmed him of the evil and treachery that might be awaiting him. He struggled emotionally as he tried to put Paula at the forefront of his mind.

"I wish Paula was waiting for me," he thinks to himself, *"I wonder if she would go back to Jamaica with me . . . I'm going to ask her."*

After the plane landed he quickly filed away all emotional entanglements; time to think rational and face reality. Even though Paula's plan is his objective, he knew that there might be diabolical obstacles waiting for him. But he's not afraid. Still, he plans to move stealthily.

He went to retrieve his car which he had paid a one month parking fee for, and then head for Sanctuary to see his good friend Robert. The eyes and ears of the community are there also, and if there's news, he'll get it.

Robert was teaching a karate class when Corey walked in, but he ended it . . . happy to see his friend.

CHYNA

"Corey, I am so happy to see you. Why you didn't come here for help if you're in trouble?"

"It was too personal, and it was nothing I couldn't handle by myself," he replied sheepishly.

"How about Paula, you saw her yet? She's in so much pain."

"No, I came here first. I went to Jamaica to think things through, but I couldn't get her out of my mind. I miss her like crazy."

"Not as much as she misses you, she said she would go by your house to look for you later."

"Great, I'll meet her there. Everything alright here?"

"Here, or do you mean Brooklyn?"

"Brooklyn?"

"People are looking for you Corey, I don't know why, but you need to clean up your act. I won't ask you about your business because I trust you, but I'm here for you if you need me. All you have to do is ask."

"I know that, and I appreciate you. But I'm good. I just want to see Paula and make things right with her, and then we can move on and put my whole past behind me."

"Clearly you're beginning to understand her love for you. I was once like you Corey, young and full of life. Felt invincible, like I could conquer the world and every one in it. I did things my way; take what I want when I want. Girls come and go in my life, but left me still wanting. Somehow, no matter how much fun we seemed to be having we never get satisfied. When I met Suzie and fell in love I started to realize there's much more to life than running around having fun. Man needs a purpose, man needs to love and be loved. You know I was never a religious person, but seeing Suzie living by her faith inspired me daily and I did my best not to disappoint her. Love is the principle that binds us together, and it was enough to overcome any obstacles that threatened us. I believe Paula is your Suzie and you should not disappoint her. Sanctuary is my purpose, and I hope one day you'll make it your purpose too. Don't stand alone if you don't have to. I have a lot of resources and they can be yours, but I can't help you if you keep me in the dark."

Corey listened attentively, and appeared to be contemplating whether or not to tell Robert everything he's involved in. Robert waited patiently, hoping that he would. But Corey just exhaled and calmly said,

CHYNA

"Everything is good except for me and Paula, and I will go and fix that now. I will make her my Suzie and love her with all that I am."

Robert smiled, still a bit concerned, but believed love has the power to overcome any problem, and heal any wound. He hugged him and gave him his blessings.

"You will do good . . . go get your Suzie and make life what you want it. Make her happy and you will be happy."

"Thank you, I will, and I want you to give me away at our wedding."

"I wouldn't have it any other way, I consider you my son Corey," Robert said, overwhelmed with emotion as his eyes welled with tears.

"Oh . . . keep these for me," Corey said as he handed Robert a folder, "I've written some poems while I was in Jamaica. You can read them and tell me what you think."

"Okay, be careful."

"I will . . . see you later," Corey replied and rushed out hoping to find Paula.

TOO YOUNG TO DIE

Robert Smith looked proud, and he expected great things from Corey. Over the years he had taught him to be strong, disciplined, and virtuous. Seeing that he is safe, and about to enter a very responsible stage of his life . . . the same stage that had made the difference in his own life made him feel delighted. He reclined in his chair and opened the folder to read the first poem:

CULTURE SHOCK

So you don't like the way I talk,

The way I dress, look, or walk.

Discard your ignorance,

And embrace the difference,

Because there is a consequence,

To discrimination, hatred, and malevolence.

So I talk, walk, dress, and look different . . . weird?

You talk, walk, dress, and look different . . . admired!

I see differences in you, as you see in me,

But in order to co-exist in a society,

We need to have tolerance and integrity.

CHYNA

Culture is the sum of knowledge, morals and beliefs,

Laws and customs that should end all strifes.

Some customs of my culture may look strange to another,

But yours is not the standard by which the world should measure.

Wake up! It's time to discard petty differences,

Wise up! We need to preserve our existence.

TOO YOUNG TO DIE

CHAPTER 15

It's about nine, and darkness begins to creep in as Corey speeds toward his house. Paula should be there soon, and he wanted to be there to welcome her. He's planning to convince Paula to run away with him to Jamaica and start a new life, a life of sun and fun . . . holding hands while walking on white sandy beaches, eating exotic tropical fruits, and listening to sweet reggae music every day. Those wonderful thoughts put hope in his heart and a smile on his face as he parked and looked around hoping to see Paula. But it appeared he's early, so he went inside and began packing some clothes while he waited.

CHYNA

TOO YOUNG TO DIE

It was exactly nine o' clock when the doorbell rang and Corey was overwhelmed with joy. He raced to the door beaming with excitement. At last, the love of his life is here and he's ready to tell her everything she wants to hear. There happiness is in reach!

He opened the door and stood in disbelief, stunned to see who was at the door.

"I called your hotel this afternoon and they said you checked out. They told me you flew back to the States and I convinced them to give me your address. I just had to find you Corey, I couldn't stop thinking about you," Sherene said franticly.

Corey, still dazed, just stood in the doorway speechless. *"Paula will be here any moment now,"* he's thinking, *"What should I do?"*

"Corey, I have something terrible to tell you, that's why I'm really here. I'm . . . " but before she could finish her sentence she fell into his arms, then a car screeched off and Corey noticed his nemesis, Lou, with a gun and a grin staring at him. He had just shot her in the back. There was no sound because his gun had on a silencer.

CHYNA

Corey pulled her inside and began crying, "I'm so sorry," he sobbed.

"It's not your fault," she muttered, "I came to warn you. Meeting you in Jamaica was part of their plan. I was supposed to drug you, or lure you back. But I fell for you instead . . . I love you," she said with her last breath. And Paula just happened to come through the door to witness with her own two eyes, the worst case scenario.

"I love you too," Corey said and kissed her, "please don't leave me," he continued as he embraced Sherene's lifeless body.

Paula had seen and heard enough. She had come in happy and excited, but now her heart is not just broken again, but shattered. She dropped the poem she had in her hand, turned around and walked out with tears in her eyes. Those words she had just heard were supposed to be hers . . . and hers only. She felt betrayed again.

Corey didn't see Paula, because he was too busy trying to ease Sherene's pain. After he realized she was dead he gently laid her on the floor and screamed out in agony.

Corey's heart is racing, so is his mind. Every misdeed he had ever done is replaying in his mind at a rapid pace.

TOO YOUNG TO DIE

What is it that he's being punished for, why did he allow that thorn, Lou, to grow in his side? Hatred and vengeance begins to work themselves into his heart as he paced the floor thinking about his next move.

Paula is also thinking of her next move. Seemed like she's have enough of not only Corey, but also Brooklyn. Still crying, and buried in thoughts she's curled up into the back of a taxi heading for the airport.

As Corey continued to pace the floor in mental anguish he noticed the poem on the floor that he had given to Paula, and now his world seemed to really come crashing down on him. All his strength seemed to have left him as he dropped down to the floor on his knees when he realized Paula was there and may have seen him with Sherene. All sorts of questions came rushing into his mind, questions without answers.

He thinks of calling Paula, but what good would that do, there plan will have to go on the backburner again. He thinks of calling Robert, but what good would that do either, "*I can't drag him into this*," he thought, "John was the only one who could help me . . . but they killed John too. They shouldn't get away with it . . . Oh God, what should I do?" He yelled out, and then went into his closet to get his gun. He grabbed the bag of clothes he had packed earlier and rushed out the door.

"Corey!"

That annoying voice sounded familiar, and Corey stopped in his tracks with his gun drawn. The last time he had seen her she was on the other side, the side that wanted him dead.

"Amy . . . who else did they send?"

"I'm alone, and nobody sent me," she said sheepishly.

"Forgive me if I don't trust you, but you hadn't made it easy for me," Corey said.

"I know, but I'm here to help you. Where's the ring I lent you?"

"That's what this is all about, a stupid ring?"

Amy was hesitant to reply.

"Where is it?"

"Here, in my pocket," he replied and showed it to her.

"Let's return it to my father together. He's a very reasonable man."

TOO YOUNG TO DIE

"Really, and all this will go away?" Corey asked.

"I don't know, but let's start there. I will do all I can to help you."

"Why don't I believe you?"

"Because I haven't being here for you, I'm sorry."

"Okay, but I won't hesitate to use this," he replied while brandishing his gun.

"I know, because you are too young to die . . . My father will listen to me."

Corey still seemed to be reacting, following blindly the plans of his adversaries. Or is he? Maybe he just wanted a way in, and he was playing a fool to catch the wise.

All the knowledge Savant and Robert had entrusted to him seemed nonexistent. He is following Amy into what seemed like a trap, and it didn't take much to convince him.

How many of us go through each day routinely, reacting to events and settling. Then get up the next day just to do the same, and then the next? It's time to think of what you want your tomorrow to be; set a plan, and work towards achieving it. What is your purpose?

CHYNA

Corey had left Sanctuary with love on his mind, a love that had filled him with joy and gave him a purpose. Now he seemed to have lost sight of that purpose; now he's venturing back into uncertainty because he's reacting. Hatred and vengeance has gotten the better of him, it's his driving force now. They are still pulling his strings.

Corey walked closely to Amy as they neared her house at the end of a winding road which followed the contour of manicured lawns. The house was modern, and huge, and richly furnished with leather and vintage oak furniture. The judge was sitting behind a desk signing some papers when they walked in and he got up to greet Corey.

"Hi daddy, Corey wanted to return the ring to you in person," Amy said cheerfully.

"Nice to finally meet you Corey, Amy explained everything to me. I'm sorry about everything my comrades had put you through. Let me help you," The Judge said extending his hand to Corey, but Corey didn't shake his hand; he just put the ring on the desk.

"No matter how hard I tried, I cannot fathom what's going on," Corey replied bewildered.

TOO YOUNG TO DIE

"All can be forgiven and forgotten if you join us," The Judge said confidently.

"No beating around the bush with you, straight to the point, right?" Corey replied boldly.

"Exactly, time is too precious to waste, and we don't have that luxury."

"And I can stop looking over my shoulders?"

"Yes Corey . . . and if you need money, a job, or anything else, you can have it, right daddy?" Amy said looking at her father.

"Sure honey, anything he wants he can have. Starting with this ring, it can be yours if you want . . . "

"What about John? What about Sherene? Should I just forget about them too?" Courtney blurted out abruptly.

"Some things you just can't undo son. You know we could have killed you too if we wanted to. Why do you rage against a system you know nothing about? Your ignorance makes you powerless. Join us and I will open your eyes to a whole new world, a world where you can have anything you want. And I mean anything, even my daughter."

CHYNA

"I already have her . . . what I want is justice!" Corey said forcefully and pulled out his gun. The Judge fumed with rage and edged closer to Corey fearlessly while pointing into his face. "You're very courageous to stand up to me, now show some wisdom and stand down. Boy, you were handpicked since the age of thirteen. We schooled you and still you won't comply. You are dead to me. Surely you don't think you scare me with that gun. Get out now before I get angry . . . and you better prepare for the wrath that's coming, you ungrateful shmuck!" The Judge shouted vehemently, "pull the trigger or run!"

"Why?" Amy asked, facing Corey.

"He sabotaged my life! I can't ask you to go against your own father, but he's evil. And I detest evil! If anyone comes after me I'm not asking questions," Corey replied and backed out of the house, realizing they had vetted and chose him since he was a child. He remembered all the way back when he was thirteen years old, how politicians paid his way through school and gave him pocket money. All those seemingly good deeds were just a scheme to control him and use him.

The Judge picked up his phone and made a proclamation:

TOO YOUNG TO DIE

"Corey is priority! Bring him to me so I can show him what hell is!"

The war is on, and the word is spreading like wildfire. Corey against an army, but an army of whom, what, or how many? He has no idea.

Back at Sanctuary Robert had just closed up and about to enter his car when Ron and Yvonne approached him.

"Hi, we are friends of Corey, do you know where we can find him?" Yvonne asked with a smile.

"Why, is he in trouble?" Robert asked keenly. But before they could respond Ron's phone rang and he quickly answered it.

"Let's go!" Ron then said to Yvonne abruptly and they hasted back to their car.

"Hey, wait!" Robert yelled out to them, but they sped off without acknowledging him.

Robert quickly took off behind them and pulled out his cell phone and called Corey, but it went straight to voicemail. He called Paula and got voicemail too. So he trailed behind Ron and Yvonne.

CHYNA

Corey was now well on his way down the winding road away from The Judge's house when a police car stopped in front of him. His gun was tucked away, but he seemed disheveled.

"Hi, why are you roaming the streets alone so late, you live around here?" The officer asked.

"Yes sir, just down the road. I was just getting some fresh air," Corey replied calmly.

"You sure, because you look nervous, stand right there for a second," the officer said as he opened his door and got out. "Let me see some identification."

"Okay, no problem," Corey replied calmly. But then the officer swiftly pulled out his gun.

"Put your hands behind you Corey," the officer ordered forcefully.

Corey obeyed, he realized the police not only knew who he was, but might be down with the enemy.

He cuffed him, then disarmed him and pushed him into the back of the car then head for The Judge's house. He parked in the driveway and pulled Corey out of the back seat as Ron and Yvonne drove up behind. And then

TOO YOUNG TO DIE

Robert pulled up at the end of the street just in time to see them entering the house.

The time for judgement seemed to be at hand, and everyone is present. This looks like the end of the road for Corey, but at least he will finally get to see what he was up against.

They threw him on the floor and surrounded him like vultures getting ready to feast. He's consumed by anger and rage, but he's restrained and alone, feeling like he's at the end of his rope.

"You have determined your own fate by your actions and refusal to join us, and now you left us no choice but to kill you. Your death will be a symbol for stupidity. Your name will hang in places like Sanctuary as a reminder of failure . . . synonymous to naught!" The Judge proclaimed emphatically.

Ron stooped down to deride him by putting on a mask and said, "Tonight is your turn to die." Then he stood up and kissed Yvonne passionately. Horrible memories came flooding into his mind. He writhed in pain as he remembered the night Danny got killed. The mask man that shot Danny had uttered similar words to him that night, and in the same mask. Now it's clear to him that Ron is his killer, and now he is his wife's lover. Lou entered the room and the picture is becoming clearer and clearer to him. He looked at Amy, thought about Sherene, and began to realize that they had being throwing him baits all the time . . . and he was biting.

Everyone took a seat, even the police, as if they were waiting for someone else. Robert Smith is still outside, but peeking through a window and contemplating how to help Corey. He sneaked around until he found a door opened to the kitchen. Corey is still on the floor, cuffed, and with his life hanging in the balance. A phone rings out loud and The Judge pressed a button on his desk, and that bellowing voice from the dungeon growled: "His ignorance has brought him to his knees, and he has become a threat. I have no use for him now, except that we turned his failure into a spectacle so everyone who opposes us will see the fate that awaits them. Televised his death and make it as painful and gruesome as possible. Let it strike fear into their hearts!"

"The Judge is not in charge," Corey realized, and it's becoming obvious that Savant was right. "This is some sort of cult, or secret society with a sophisticated network of prominent men and women at the top, coordinating a framework of evil to control and dominate us. I've being wandering instead of living. Reacting, instead of acting . . . I've being such a fool."

TOO YOUNG TO DIE

Time is running out for Corey, and Robert realized he needs to act fast. He turned on the gas stove at full blast and sneaked back outside. He picked up a big rock and threw it into Ron's car windshield and it set off the alarm, and then quickly ran back into the kitchen.

Lou and the police ran outside, and Ron and Yvonne quickly followed behind, while The Judge and Amy watched Corey.

"Perfect," Robert thought, then attacked The Judge with a flying drop kick that sent him crashing onto his desk. Amy screamed out loud and ran upstairs.

"Robert, am I glad to see you," Corey said delightfully.

"Save it for later, we need to get out of here fast!" Robert replied. "Follow me."

They head for the kitchen but was surprised by Ron and Yvonne; but no problem, with swift kicks and karate chops to the face and body, Robert quickly rendered Ron unconscious. Yvonne crouched shamefully in a corner with Corey staring at her in disgust. Then in comes Lou rushing through the front door and Corey meet him with a drop kick to his throat. He hit the floor hard, and remained there motionless. Corey looked at Robert for a cue for what to do next, and he responded.

CHYNA

"Let's go out the back, this place could blow up any second," he said, and leads the way through the kitchen; but at the same time the officer came rushing through the front door and see them leaving. He pulled out his gun and fired.

"Boom!" The thunderous sound of the explosion rocked the neighborhood, and sent debris flying everywhere. Corey and Robert were sprawled out on the back yard lawn, but alive. They rolled over to look at the entire house up in flames and the roof all gone.

"Justice!" Corey said, still in cuffs.

Robert looked at him with a smile and said, "How did you get yourself into this mess?"

"By reacting," he replied sheepishly.

"What?" Robert asked, confused.

"Never mind, I'll explain it to you one day. Let's get out of here.

They helped each other up and blended into the crowd of onlookers. Fire trucks, ambulances and police cars raced to the scene with sirens blasting.

TOO YOUNG TO DIE

"Nobody could have survived that blast," Robert said. "Let's go to my place, we can get those handcuffs off there." Corey agreed, and they left.

The explosion seemed to have put an end to Corey's troubles, or is it the beginning? He didn't even give it a thought, he's happy to escape. Minutes ago his life was hanging in the balance with no hope of surviving, and now he feels free and elated. Lou, the thorn in his side, is removed, and nothing or no one to look over his shoulder for.

CHÝNA

CHAPTER 16

It's the dawn of a new day, and hopefully the dawn of a new life. Corey woke up feeling relieved and refreshed. A great night's sleep and a new state of mind made him feel positive about the future.

Jamaica is on his mind, and he decided to put his thoughts on paper, so he begins to write a poem:

TOO YOUNG TO DIE

JAMAICA

Jamaica, an island in the sun,

A place of immeasurable fun,

The bounty of nature exemplified,

Jamaica is always on my mind.

Falls, springs, rivers and beaches,

Reggae, fruits, birds and fishes,

Colorful people with a colorful culture,

Destined to have a glorious future.

Out of many, one people,

How uncanny, but admirable,

Black, Chinese, White and Indian,

Living in ease, united as one.

I love you, oh how I'm missing you,

Paradise of the world I dubbed you,

With blessings from above,

Jamaica . . . land we love.

CHYNA

Seemed like Corey is all ready to go back to Jamaica, but Paula is still missing. Now he needs to find her, he needs a purpose . . . he needs to start making life what he wants it to be. He reached for his phone and dialed Paula but it went straight to voicemail and he became agitated. Robert walked in and noticed.

"She's not answering?" He asked out of concern.

"No, if only I could get one chance to explain to her . . ."

"Don't give up on her, more importantly, don't give up on yourself. From what you told me last night, you still have some loose ends to tie up."

"Oh yeah, will you follow me?"

"Of course, I don't think this is over Corey, but before we go to the police station I think we should swing by your house."

"Okay, I think so too. I am ready if you are."

"Yeah, let's go before the kids wake up. If they see you there's no way of escaping. They've being asking about you."

Seemed like the worse is over, but Corey is still plagued by memories and apprehension. Paula is missing, last night could have monumental criminal implications, and there's a body in his house to explain. Not to mention the voice that he had heard which gave the order to kill him. Who is he, and what might he have planned next? The discomfort is obvious in his demeanor, and Robert tried to ease it.

"You should stop worrying, you didn't do anything wrong. You were just in the wrong place at the wrong time, and you did what any normal person would do. It was all about survival, and you did."

"I guess that's what it boils down to, but I could have avoided it. After Danny died I lost focus . . . I fell asleep. And you had warned me not to, remember? I could have died."

"Well, stop beating yourself up about it, the next step is to make sure you're not implicated in anyway," Robert said as they neared Corey's home.

"I think we should park here and walk the rest of the way," Corey suggested.

Everything seemed normal, the usual traffic, and several people walking their dogs. But still they inconspicuously scouted the area as they walked down the street uncertain of what they might be walking into.

CHYNA

Corey took a deep breath then opened the door . . . stunned in disbelief, and speechless, he froze. Robert walked around him to see why, but he too appeared stunned. They were expecting to see Sherene's body lying in a pool of blood, but there's no body and no blood. And why weren't the neighborhood swarming with cops?

"This is strange," Robert said, breaking the silence.

"No, it's not."

"What?" Robert asked, confused.

"It's really true, they are above the law. This is bigger than I had imagined."

"You're losing me Corey, bodies don't just disappear."

"Let's go, I'll tell you about it in the car," Corey said as he led the way out of the house.

Corey was schooled by Savant, but he didn't quite grasp the significance and magnitude of the wisdom he was given. Now it's making sense to him.

"There's this secret society, well, they're not exactly secret, because they will accept anyone, and sometimes operate in the open. What is secret about them is their nature and their deceptive ways. They are in powerful places Robert, politicians, judges, lawyers, police, you name it. They are well organized and right now I feel like a dead man walking."

"If that's true, then we can't go to the police. Either we find a way to fight them or you'll have to disappear."

"I don't want to leave without Paula."

"Maybe it's better to just leave her alone. You don't want this to affect her."

"You're right, I'm just going to lay low for a while and see what happens next. I really don't want to run, there's nowhere to hide. They had found me when I was in Jamaica."

"You can stay with me as long as you want."

"I know, but I can't, your family will be in danger."

"Corey, you are family," Robert replied as they pulled up in front of Sanctuary.

"You know what I mean . . . I have somewhere to stay, but I'll keep in touch."

CHYNA

"Okay, whatever you think is best. Anything you need just let me know. By the way, I read your poems and they are great. You really have talent."

"Thanks, writing makes me feel free, so when I need to get away that's what I do."

"Do you mind if I let Suzie read them?"

"By all means, and tell me what she thinks of them."

"Okay, call me later and tell me where you're staying."

"I will . . . thank you for everything," Corey said emotionally and drove off.

Now Corey Young is alone again, heading into the uncertain world he's becoming accustom to. Without Paula there's no purpose, and without purpose he's destined to fall back into the daily routine of reacting again: like a fish biting at baits thrown his way. So far he was lucky not to get hooked, but how long before the right bait comes along and really snag him?

One's desire to seek pleasure, fame, or money, can cause him to experiment and taste all kinds of enticements dangling before his eyes. Without a strong foundation of moral values he can get trapped in a system that demands his very soul; a system where the players methods are deceptive, dangerous and unethical.

Corey Young no longer seem to be driven by pleasure nor money, nor is he seeking fame. But without a purpose, and a past that still haunts him it's easy to stumble in the wake of last night's events. He is roaming without a compass, no direction or information. He is like a lost soul wandering and waiting to react . . . the same mistake he made before. He entertained the thought of running back to Jamaica but remembered they will know where to find him. The only thought that eased his anxiety is the one of Paula, so he relished in her memories to save his sanity as he cruised down the FDR Drive on his way to Battery Park.

CHÝNA

CHAPTER 17

Battery Park is a 25-acre public park at the southern tip of Manhattan Island in New York City. It is a peaceful place where you can just relax and enjoy the sun. You can also stare at the Statue of Liberty from there to get a sense of freedom. Maybe that's why Corey is there, he's on a bench staring at the Statue of Liberty in wonderment. Suddenly he pulled out his phone and called Savant.

"Greetings brethren," he answered happily. "You need a taxi?"

"Maybe soon, but not right now, I'm in big trouble and I have no clues what to do," Corey replied anxiously.

TOO YOUNG TO DIE

"Okay, did it have anything to do with that ring?"

"Everything!"

"Don't say another word. I'm going to text you an address and a name right now. Go and see him as soon as you can and he will help you. Tell him I sent you, he's my uncle."

"Are you sure, because people are getting killed."

"Good bye Corey, go see him now!" he replied strongly, and hang up the phone.

Corey waited for the text which came in less than two minutes. And then he jumped into his car and heads for Savant's uncle. He had no idea what kind of help to expect, but anything is better than nothing.

As he got close to the address he slowed down to look for the building, which turned out to be a church.

'A church, wow, he sent me to see a priest,' He thought.

He parked, looked around, and then walked through the big front door of the church which was slightly opened.

CHYNA

"Hello," he called out loud, but the only response he got was the echo of his own voice, and then he heard footsteps. He waited patiently until a tall bearded man dressed like a monk emerged from the shadows.

"Hello, welcome to the house of God," he said with a friendly voice.

"Good evening, I'm Corey, and I'm looking for Mr. Henry."

"You've found him, what can I do for you?"

"Savant sent me to see you."

"Oh yes, follow me to my office," he replied with a smile and turned back to where he had come from. Corey followed him into a small office decorated with ancient religious artefacts and paintings.

"Savant had told me about your plight, which is common, but not many understand what they are involved into. For me to help you I need to know how you feel about everything that's being happening to you. Can you be honest with me?"

"I will, Savant told me I could trust you, and I can see that you are a man of God," Corey replied, barely smiling.

TOO YOUNG TO DIE

"I'm hoping it's not my attire or this building that you will eventually draw your conclusions from . . . tell me about the terrible things you're involved in and how they made you feel."

"I came to America as a teenager, and literally grew up on the streets of Brooklyn. I got mixed up with bad company and did a lot of bad things, but I met a wonderful girl and fell in love. Since then I stopped hanging out with the guys and thought about getting married and start a family, but after my best friend got killed I somehow lost focus and start gambling and hanging out with bad company again; which got me involved with some real evil people. They tried to get me to join a group, but I was always suspicious about it, and now, people are dying all around me and I could be next. I feel guilty, even though I know I'm not all responsible. I'm tired of running!"

"The mere fact that you feel guilty is a good sign that you are already saved; in other words, if you weren't saved your sin would not bother you. I'm not going to try to impress you with words of man's wisdom, as the great apostle Paul would say. But I'm going to talk to your spirit, and if you don't understand me then you don't have the spirit. Let's start with your addiction . . . "

CHYNA

"I don't have one!" Corey interjected sharply.

"Okay, who am I to judge you? Drugs and alcohol aren't the only addiction, and addiction is one way of keeping you into mental slavery. Once addicted, that addiction becomes your purpose, everything you do revolves around it, and you become oblivious to everything else happening around you. You will neglect your real purpose. All sin is of the flesh, and because we were born of the flesh there is sin in us. Man is a threefold being, spirit, soul, and this body which is the flesh. Corey, you often find yourself doing bad things that you don't want to do, right?" Mr. Henry asked.

"Exactly, that's when I feel terrible," Corey replied.

"Give me an example."

"Lying . . . or cheating on my girlfriend."

"You do them often?"

Corey was hesitant to answer, and appeared chagrined. Mr. Henry sounded just like Savant, as if they had learned from the same source, only, Mr. Henry was more religious.

"You don't have to answer. When you commit a sin and you feel guilty you struggle with that emotion because of your spirit. *'For I know that nothing good dwells in me, that is, in my flesh. For I have the desire to do what is right, but not the ability to carry it out.'* Romans 7:18. *'But there is another power within me that is at war with my mind. This power makes me a slave to the sin that is still within me.'* Romans 7:23. They will try to entice you into their way of life, with sex, drugs, fame, and money, which you did to some degree, and to join their club, which you refused. They are running out of options, so now they want you to sink so deep into sin that your guilt will make you feel worthless and hopeless, to the point that you will become evil as they are. This is when your conscience doesn't bother you. Have you ever being baptized Corey?"

"Yes, when I was about fifteen. I used to go to church regular when I was in Jamaica, but since I came to America only once or twice a year."

"Yeah, so much distraction pulling us every which way, your spirit has sustained you. The battle you are fighting is already won, and all you have to do is accept the victory. Satan cannot harm you unless you give him the power and the means. Every sin you commit is an open invitation to him to come into your life to do as he's please. Whoever you think you are at war with answers to Satan. He is the true leader of that group or secret society that they want you to join. Those groups or institutions are all over the world under many different names, and sometimes they use religion to camouflage their true nature. But they have one master, Satan. Many of their members don't even know who they are serving. So how do you stop him from attacking you? Simple, just stop giving him invitations and stop reacting to his methods. *"Submit yourselves therefore to God. Resist the devil and he will flee from you."* James 4:7. Jesus Christ fasted forty days and forty nights before facing Satan in an epic battle of spiritual will, Mathew 4:2. Deny the flesh all the sinful crave that you might have, and work on your spirit man. Start with reading the Bible, that's how you feed and strengthen the spirit. Sin is food for the flesh, and the Word is food for the spirit. Jesus said, *"It is the Spirit who gives life; the flesh profits nothing; the words that I have spoken to you are spirit and are life."* John 6:63. Amen."

"I get it . . . I do understand what you're saying. And maybe I had more than one addiction. Thinking back, I believe lust and money sometimes clouded my judgement, and when I made a mistake I might have lied or resorted to some other sin to cover or justify my actions. It was like a domino effect just tumbled out of control . . . and here I am."

"It's not over, and it will be a constant struggle, because the devil is cunning. If you are doing his bidding ignorantly he'll leave you to die in your sins. If you dance with him you will definitely die in your sins. That's his goal. But resist him and he will flee from you. The bottom line is that your soul is at stake. No matter what happens next . . . Do not react . . . that's how he keep you enslaved. *"Vengeance is mine, I will repay, says the Lord."* Romans 12:19. The real battle is within, and you must win that battle. I still struggle from day to day because of this fleshly body that I live in, and I know this struggle will never end until I'm free of this body. But as long as I live in this physical world I will have to contend with this physical body. Remember, sin is an open invitation, and there is a spiritual and a physical consequence. What a man, in his natural state cannot see he cannot understand, or even think about; out of sight out of mind. Now, when you become enlightened you are beyond natural, you are able to see, understand, and think spiritually."

"I will remember, thank you. I can see much more clearly now, and I know what I must do. I would love to come back and talk with you more . . . there's so much I need to learn," Corey said humbly.

"Jesus Christ had a purpose and he stayed true to it, He didn't react to Satan's lies, deceptions, and other evil methods. Find your purpose!"

"I definitely will," Corey replied and shook his hand, and Mr. Henry walked with him all the way out to the front door.

Enlightened with a new and better sense of his true enemy, Corey is confident that he can survive this game the devil is playing with his life. His best plan is Paula's plan, but first he'll have to find Paula. And as he drove off he called her on his cell phone, but it went straight to voicemail again.

No sense in leaving another message, she hadn't returned any of his calls or respond to any of his messages. Surprisingly though, he didn't looked discouraged or sad. He turned on the radio and began singing along with the song playing as he cruised through the streets of Brooklyn with a renewed sense of purpose.

TOO YOUNG TO DIE

CHAPTER 18

It's only six in the evening, but the overcast sky made it look like nine, and very gloomy, but Corey appeared somewhat elated. His mind was now clear and free, and he understood who his enemy was. He now realized the people he had rumbled with from day to day weren't his real enemies, and that they were just as blind as he was; puppets on strings reacting to the puppet master's directions. What a difference the truth can make, but according to Mr. Henry, not everyone is receptive to the truth. He had told Corey he wouldn't speak to him with words of man's wisdom. That would not have helped him. He would still be stumbling in the dark. He told him he would speak to his spirit and if he understood, that meant he was already saved and could come out of the dark into the light. *"The way of the wicked is like darkness: They do not know what makes them stumble,"* Proverbs 4:19. *"For you have delivered me from death and my feet from stumbling, that I may walk before God in light of life,"* Psalm 56:13. Corey seemed spiritually enlightened, and now he has the right perspective on life; but to what degree, and for how long? Only time will tell!

Corey's car came to a screeching halt right in front of Paula's house, and he hopped out and ran to the door.

"Paula! Paula! Paula!" He yelled as he pounded on the door repeatedly. The door opened and Paula's mother stood in the doorway.

"Sorry Corey, she's gone, my baby is gone," she sobbed.

"She didn't tell you where?"

TOO YOUNG TO DIE

"She went to live with her father in Florida, maybe it's best for her . . . I don't know, but I miss her so much. You drove her away."

"I know, but I'll make things right . . . I promise," Corey replied as his eyes welled up with tears.

"She loves you so much, why did you have to hurt her so much?"

"I didn't mean to, I wish I could undo it all, but I can't. But I'll figure out a way to make things right because I love her too, and she means everything to me."

"Be careful son, and don't give up on her . . . I think she just need some time away."

"I'll keep in touch, take care of yourself," Corey said and hopped back into his car.

At least he knew Paula was safe, away from this treacherous environment. Now he needs to get away himself and join Paula, but first he decided to stop by and see his good friend Robert Smith. Sanctuary is still open, and he could have one of those one on one lectures with him, but this time he wanted to impart some wisdom to Robert. Robert Smith was a good man, but not a spiritual man, and so all the knowledge he had bestowed on Corey now seemed superficial. Corey, in his enlightenment realized Robert never saw the big picture, at least from outside the box. He had taught him the virtues of a good man, how to be strong and resilient, but he never understood the true essence of a man. Man is more than what you see with your physical eyes, man has a spirit that knows how to overcome the flesh, that part of man that makes him so wretched; and he's excited that he can explain that to his good friend and mentor.

As Corey turned down the street he noticed Robert getting into his car and he sped up to catch him . . . then boom! Robert's car exploded in flames amidst a thunderous sound. Corey screeched to a halt and rushed out of his car to help, but there was nothing he could do. Amidst the debris and clouds of thick black smoke still hovering in the air, Robert Smith's lifeless body laid bloodied. Corey stooped over him in tears, then looked up into the heavens and screamed.

"Why! Why! Why!"

A crowd of people gathered, but kept their distance as the blaring sounds of sirens raced to the scene. Corey struggled to get to his feet, he felt weak and helpless, alone and desolate.

TOO YOUNG TO DIE

"*It's not over*," he thought, as he walked fraily back to his car and somehow managed to speed off through the traffic of police cars and firetrucks. In four minutes he was at Robert's house and fully recovered physically. He ran to the door and pounded on it, and Mrs. Smith answered quickly.

"What is it Corey?" She asked sternly.

"Something terrible happened, Robert is dead," he cried.

"Oh God, tell me you're joking," she said, frightened.

"His car blew up with him. I think somebody planted a bomb in it."

"Why would somebody do that? He didn't do anything to anybody," she said crying.

"No . . . I think it's because of me. I got mixed up with some very bad people and he helped me out. I'm so sorry, it's my fault."

Corey seemed to be losing his bearings as he banged his head on the wall and cried profusely. Mrs. Smith is still crying too as she searched for her car keys.

CHYNA

"I'm going to see him; you'll have to stay here with the kids until I get back, they are already sleeping."

"No . . . I can't, association with me is like the kiss of death. Too much people are dying around me, and I don't want to put you guys in any more danger."

"Corey . . . please, I need to do this," she pleaded.

"Okay, be careful," these evil people are just roaming the streets with malign intentions. They must be stopped," he replied and hugged her,

What next, will Corey succumb to his emotions and react, will he just run and hide, or are there other options he's contemplating? He's obviously writhing in pain. His face looked contorted as he paced the floor with his hands on his head.

How often does one sunk into psychosis, or turned to violent and evil indulgences because they don't have a strong resolve. Corey seemed to be vacillating on the edge of moral collapse, thinking of vengeance in the worse ways. All the wisdom from Robert, Henry, and Savant seemed forgotten or nonexistent. He writhed in pain and cried in shame without relief, but sleep came to his aide once again, and he passed out in the sofa.

TOO YOUNG TO DIE

CHAPTER 19

It is dawn, and the memories of last night crept in and prompted Corey to jump out of his sleep. He yawned and opened his eyes to see Robert's wife sitting across from him sobbing, and he began to cry again.

"I'm so sorry, if there's anything I can do just let me know," he said softly.

"You'll have to carry on his work at Sanctuary, Robert said you would be the only one capable to," she replied.

CHYNA

"I know . . . my head feels like it's going to explode right now. I don't know where I'm going to start from."

"Don't worry about it; just take it one day at a time."

"I'm talking about the people that killed him, I can't let them get away with it," Corey replied angrily.

"Son, they won't . . . leave it to God," she replied calmly.

"Okay, I need to go see my mother. Call me if you need me," Corey said and hugged her.

"I'm serious Corey, leave it to God. You have so much to live for, and a lot of people are depending on you now."

"I know . . . I'll come back later to see if there's anything you need me for. I'll stop by Sanctuary and make sure everything is fine there."

"Okay, Robert loved you . . . we all love you!"

"I know, and I love you guys too," he replied, still crying.

Corey walked out the door feeling guilty. His association with Robert caused him his life, and thoughts of vengeance begin to creep in again.

TOO YOUNG TO DIE

He might have had a good spirit, but he was still in the flesh, and the all too familiar struggle began to take root in his mind again. As he drove down the street he thought about Paula, the only person who could give him real comfort, but she's nowhere around. He thought about John, but they had killed him too. He looked down at the gun in his lap and his blood begins to boil.

"Let God handle it, Suzie had no idea. Vengeance is the only fitting justice," he was thinking. But vengeance on whom, and where will he start? Then he thought about what he had learned from Savant and his uncle, Mr. Henry; and so he began to realize he's reacting, just like his enemy wanted him to. That old serpent, called the Devil, and Satan, which deceiveth the whole world.

In the beginning Robert Smith did counseled Corey about the cycle of treacherous manipulation of mankind under the wheels of diverse political systems and their injustices that was put in place long ago to indoctrinate and control, using their curriculum to shape the type of life they wanted certain members of society to live; and not to get trapped in a life of conformity. But now he realized that there is a dark and greater force at the helm with an infernal goal, which Robert didn't fully understand.

CHYNA

"I'm playing into the devil's hand . . . they're still pulling my strings. No more! No more!" He blurted out. And then suddenly he pulled over by the Brooklyn Bridge and tossed his gun into the East river, and immediately that mysterious burden, his anger and thoughts of hatred and vengeance vanished; and he began to fully understand that his mental state was a result of his emotional and physical reactions to events. *"Mr. Henry was right, and the Bible he quoted the scriptures from is right and must be the infallible truth of The Creator. The Spirit is the key to win this battle over the flesh. For I know that in me, that is in my flesh, nothing good dwells."* What did Corey seem to get, and what do we all need?

REDEMPTION !!!

TOO YOUNG TO DIE

CHAPTER 20

    As the days passed by Corey helped Mrs. Smith with the preparations of Robert's funeral, but he spent most of his days and nights at his mother's house thinking and evaluating the recent events that had placed him into his present condition. The news had broadcast about The Judge's mansion being blown up from a gas leak, but no mention of bodies being found, odd, but not surprising.

Everything seemed quiet on the home front though, no more incidents, only mental assimilations. He reflected all the way back to Danny's death. All the incidents and invitations to get him to join that mystery group were implicit, but all the wisdom from Savant and Mr. Henry was explicit. One led to death, and the other to life.

We have reached unprecedented heights of innovative and technological accomplishments, knowledge is abounding . . . and we are having fun. Many of us are indulging in sexual immorality, alcohol, violence, and drugs, without limits. But behind the glamour and decadence of that lifestyle lies a diabolical plot to drag us into the abyss of hell. The question is: Is it worth it?

Corey appeared to have made the right choice, even though he struggled because of his weaknesses. We all have weaknesses, of which lies within our flesh, but we also have the power within, our spirit, to overcome those weaknesses. It's a matter of choice and discipline! Corey made is choice, but how disciplined is he, and how strong is his new found faith? Only time can tell!

TOO YOUNG TO DIE

Other books written by Chyna are available at Barnes & Nobles, and on Amazon and Kindle:

Redemption, by Chyna

The Jamerican, by Chyna

Heartfelt Cries, by Chyna

Moral Discipline, by Chyna

You can contact Chyna on Facebook, Twitter, Instagram, and Yahoo mail at:
chyna.chin@yahoo.com

Phone #: (941) 249-0054

Google: Chynachin

ACKNOWLEDGEMENTS

All glory to my Redeemer, Lord and Savior Jesus Christ. And special thanks to my greatest blessings: Sandra,

Chynna, and Jordon Lue, and Indya Jade Chatman. I would also like to acknowledge the following people, who at some point on my very adventurous journey through life, somehow made an indelible impact:

Gerard Agard, Nakia Anderson, Nicola Barnes, Tanyia Bowlding, Andrea Brown, Annmarie Brown, Delly-Ann Brown, Kimberly Byfield, Cornelia Clarke, Althea Clemmings, Andrea Daley, Michka Daughma, Jhanelle Dormevil, Patricia Edwards, Richard Embden, Desereen Evelyn, Rilla Fairman, Angella Garvey, Desmond Garvey, Gary Garvey, Ingrid Garvey, Lloyd Garvey, Nadine Garvey, Nerrisa Garvey, Norman Garvey, Wayne Garvey, Wendy Garvey, Monica Graison, Kim Harrison, Marc Herouard, Chanalee Johnson, Deehan Williams-Johnson, Honiball Johnson, Francine Kelly, Latoya Johnson, Louis Lewis, Carmen Lloyd, Trevor Lloyd, Anna-Kay Lue, Chiney Lue, Keisha Lue, Kevin Lue, Marcia Lue, Maxie Lue, Monique Lue, Wendy Lue, Duval Lynch, Wayne Lyttleton, Leila Mason, Kimberly Graison-McBride, Osciantwi McDonald, Lisa McFarlane, Keisha McHayle, Daphne Mesilas, Icesis Ashley Miller, Champagne Miller, Travis Miller, Byron Muthra, Rotilda Muthra, Sacha Parchment, Sherrika Parchmon, Derrick Phillips, Kim Phillips, Tracy Piper, Rudeboy Reidy, Pauline Richards, Paula Stewart, Kenisha Thompson, Camellia Walker, Oral Walker, Vanria Walker, Norma Watson, and Winston Watson.

CHÝNA

A special thanks to

Beatrice Kubenik-Erlwein,

a very dear friend, a beautiful soul,

and one of my greatest inspiration.

www.ingramcontent.com/pod-product-compliance
Lightning Source LLC
Chambersburg PA
CBHW071340280526
45787CB00001B/156